our world

the official book written with the full co-operation of boyzone

eddie rowley

EBURY
PRESS

First published in Great Britain in 1998

1 3 5 7 9 10 8 6 4 2

Ebury Press
Random House, 20 Vauxhall Bridge Road, London SW1V 2SA

Random House Australia Pty Limited
20 Alfred Street, Milsons Point, Sydney, New South Wales 2061, Australia

Random House New Zealand Limited
18 Poland Road, Glenfield, Auckland 10, New Zealand

Random House South Africa (Pty) Limited
Endulini, 5A Jubilee Road, Parktown 2193, South Africa

Random House UK Limited Reg. No. 954009

A CIP catalogue record for this book is available from the British Library

ISBN 0 09 186488 7

Design and reproduction by Blackjacks, London

Photography by **Philip Ollerenshaw** except, Ulli Schanz pp.6, 20, 40, 78;
Piers Allardyce pp.68 (top right) and 71; Ulf Magnusson p.79 (right);
Denis O'Regan p.85; Dave Willis p.86 (top left);
Tim Roney p.86 (bottom left); Ray Burmiston p.87.
All photographs supplied by Idols Licensing and Publicity Ltd © 1998

Printed and bound in Great Britain by Butler & Tanner Ltd, Frome

Papers used by Ebury Press are natural, recyclable products
made from wood grown from sustainable forests.

introduction

So much has happened in the Boyzone camp since our last book, *Living The Dream*. When we stop and take stock of the events in our lives, it seems impossible that five guyz could have had such an eventful year, as you will read when you delve into *Boyzone Our World*.

We left off the last book at 'Picture of You' and since then we've had so many individual experiences and landmarks in our lives, both on and off the stage. There have been good times and bad. Thankfully, most of the occurrences have been happy ones.

Ronan has had to deal with the death of his dear Mum. Only those who have lost a parent can truly understand the agony and desolation it brings. But he battled through the grief to find happiness with his beautiful wife, Yvonne, who is an Irish model.

We've been around the world again and with such busy lives as pop performers you'd think there would be no time for a life away from the stage. But Shane and Easther also tied the knot and Mikey signalled his intentions in that direction by becoming engaged to Sharon.

While other groups have gone their separate ways or experienced major changes, thank God Boyzone have stuck together as a team and we seem to be getting stronger and stronger. We are so thrilled to have hit the number one spot in the charts again in 1998. Please God, as long as you the fans stick by us, Boyzone will continue to be top of the pops. We hope you enjoy this book and hopefully you will know the real Boyzone even better at the end of it.

lots of love

Keith

God Bless Ro

Take Care

God Bless Steve

Enjoy yourself

Mike xxx

it's a balmy Sunday afternoon at the beginning of summer 1998 and Stephen Gately is lost in his own world, enjoying the tranquillity of the dead calm sea in a boat off the coast of Dublin.

Away from the showbiz spotlight and the frenzied activity that goes with his life as a member of Boyzone, Steve grabs the opportunity to relax in peaceful surroundings. The young pop idol loves the ocean and his dream is to own a home that runs on to a beach. From the vantage point of his boat, Steve can spot U2 superstar Bono's magnificent white mansion overlooking picturesque Killiney Bay on the south side of Dublin city.

It's set in a stunning residential belt that includes the picture postcard village of Dalkey and is favoured by stars of entertainment and sport. Apart from Bono, Enya lives there, as does Jim Kerr of Simple Minds and Grand Prix ace Damon Hill. Steve admits his dream is to put down his roots in the area when his life slows down.

It's a world away from Stephen's origins in the tough inner city of Dublin around Sheriff Street and Seville Place. But as he returns to the humble three-bed terraced house on a long street where he grew up with his three brothers and one sister, the memories that come flooding back are happy ones.

'There were seven of us in that house, including Mum and Dad, and we used to have a laugh when we were kids,' Steve recalls. 'We used to play games out in the back garden, climb the walls, fall off the walls, loads of games that kids play. We used to kill each other half the time. Just stupid, ridiculous things.

'The road is named after a priest, Canon Ellis, who preached in the area and the story goes that he wasn't one of the nicest priests. He was real strict and he used to scold the kids. They say that his ghost still walks up and down the street. We have had many different doors on the front of our house. We used to have a blue one, which was very distinctive. My Da loves doing things differently.

'I used to share a room with my brothers Mark and Alan. In the evenings we'd play out on the green, do our homework, watch some TV or chat about what went on during the day before going to bed. When I come home now I still clean up, tidy up for my Ma and help my Dad cook the dinner. But I spend most of the time chatting because I'm always away, so there's a lot of catching up on things happening in their lives and my life.'

As he drives around the area where he grew up, Stephen stops outside the North Strand Vocational School and laughs as he tells you how he used to practise signing his autograph there as a pupil in preparation for life as a star. He says, 'I was thirteen or fourteen years of age and I used to sign my autograph all the time. All day, every day, just signing my autograph. I remember saying to two of my classmates, Keith and Wesley, "In a few years, this autograph will be worth something. When I'm older this will be worth money." And they looked at me as if I was mad. Two years ago, I met them in town and I completely forgot about this and one of the guys came up to me and said, "You were right. I remember you saying to me when you were signing your autograph that you were going to be famous. And you were right." School was a great time. I had no problems in school. I was never picked on in the school, never ever in all my classes. The first day I went there I decided I was going breeze through secondary school or else I'd go through it the hard way. I was determined that I wouldn't go through five years of being picked on or being bullied. So I picked on the biggest guy and we had a scrap and I came out on top, luckily, thank God. He was a big fellow, so I got respect from that and I never had a problem afterwards. I haven't seen him since I left school. His name is Stephen as well.

'I loved school and I got on well with all the teachers, but not in a sense of being teacher's pet...just that I got on well. I always had a laugh, I did my work and I loved art, science and English. They were my favourite subjects.

'That's where I started off doing drama, doing acting. I joined a drama group. I studied drama in school as well with a lovely teacher named Miss Higgins. She is so happy the way things worked out for me. She was always telling me brother, "Tell Stephen I was asking for him."

'My brother Tony is still there, he's the youngest. Every now and again I try to get back and go in and say hello to the teachers, although it's changed because there are a lot of new teachers there now. But it's a place that brings back memories every time I drive by. There's a big tree outside and from my science class I could see the tree, see the leaves falling off, the snow falling on it, new leaves, all the seasons. That always sticks in my mind going by that school. The tree is still there.

'It's lovely to go back and see my art class. The teacher still has one of my pictures up on display. They are all really proud of what I've done. I remember when I was in the North Strand, the teachers were always giving lectures about the past pupils who had done really, really well and I was thinking how I wanted the Principal to say the same about me after I'd left school and gone on to achieve something big. I always wanted that.

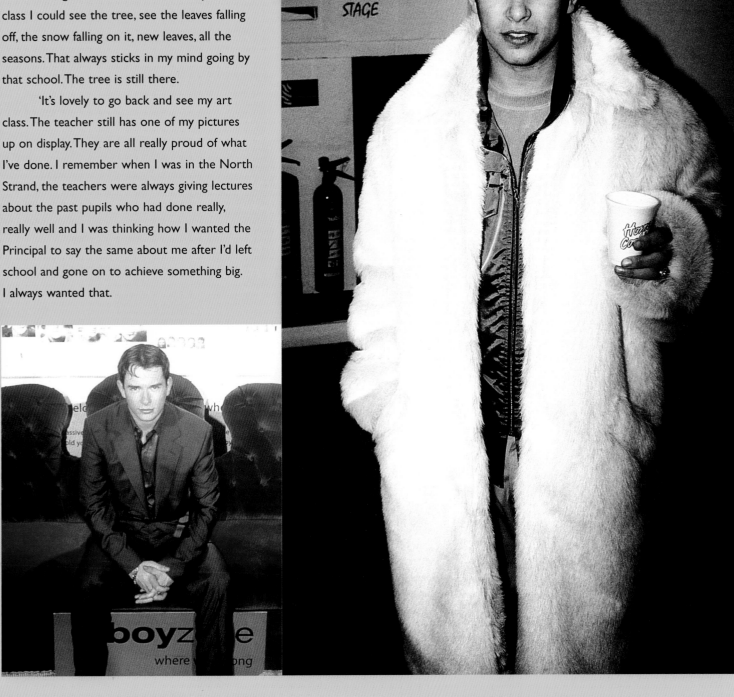

'My ambitions when I was there were to do with the entertainment world, ever since I was young. I didn't know I was going to end up in the music side, in a pop group. But I knew I was definitely going to do something in the entertainment business whether it was singing, acting, dancing. I did modelling as a kid. I was too small, so I didn't know what I was going to do. But as long as it was one of those four things, just anything in the entertainment business. I went for audition after audition for films, auditions for Neil Jordan, auditions for Alan Parker, films that they did. It's just mad how things turned out.'

As he pulls up outside the North Strand Bowling Alley, Stephen says, 'In my early teens, I spent a lot of my time in that bowling alley. I'd meet up with all me mates and have a laugh. We'd spend the whole night there. It had one of the first quasar games in Ireland and I used to go there all the time and play. There was a restaurant and we'd sit around and it was a bit like the movie *Grease*. I was watching *Grease* the other night and it was a bit like that, hanging out with all your mates and there were different gangs there.'

The O'Connell's Boys Club also holds fond memories for Stephen, so he was disappointed to discover that it's now closed down. 'It looks as if there's nothing there now,' he says. 'It was run by a guy called Mr Gal. I think it was Mr Gallagher, but we just called him Mr Gal. He was a lovely gentleman, really tall, wore glasses, he was like a teacher. There must have been about forty of us at one stage in the club and it was great because you could go sailing. I love sailing. I used to sail out in Dun Laoghaire for three years with the local club there and I used to do canoeing and mountain climbing.

I used to go swimming every Friday night and I remember how the instructor was a really old woman, but so incredibly fit. She had a little bit of a lisp and every time she talked we'd crack up laughing, as you do when you're kids. One of the guys one day had something wrong with his leg. She said, "It's a spaassssm," and the whole place just erupted with laughter. She didn't care, she knew we'd take the mickey. That was a good club. All my mates out of school used to go there: Trevor, David, Michael, Derek and Stephen Maher. The whole load of us used to hang around up there. It was just a nice place to get away.

'We used to play hide and seek there. I was quite small and one day I hid in a canoe and the guys put something on top of the canoe and I couldn't get out. I was stuck there for about half an hour and I was calling out, but they wouldn't let me out. They knew I was there, but they wouldn't let me out. Just little things like that. Then we played tricks on other people. It was good and if it's gone it's a shame, it was great for kids around my area.'

The Point Depot in Dublin's dock-lands is Ireland's top pop and live entertainment venue. Last year's Eurovision Song Contest, which Ronan co-hosted and Boyzone sang 'Let The Message Run Free' during the interval, was staged in The Point's indoor arena.

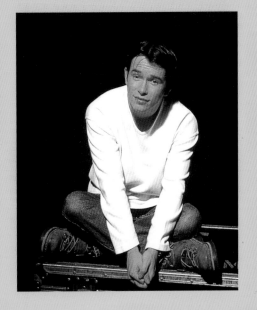

The world's top acts, including U2, Take That, The Spice Girls and All Saints have all performed there. Once again, Boyzone will end their autumn/winter tour there this Christmas. But during the summer as Stephen returned to the old haunts of his teenage years and stopped outside The Point, he had a confession to make: 'When we were kids years ago we used to go down to The Point and gatecrash concerts there. One of our mates would have a ticket for a concert, he'd go in and we'd be outside, then he'd push open the doors and we'd all run in and the security would run for us. Three or four might get away and the rest would be caught, the rest would be thrown out again. So at least four of us got in without paying. I remember one of the concerts I gatecrashed was MC Hammer.

'I never had money at that time. It was just one of the tricks and games that kids would do to get away with things. My parents hadn't got major money. Somebody would have a ticket and that's how we used to go in. It's a gas considering now I'm playing there. There's probably kids outside doing the very same thing at Boyzone concerts these days. It's great if they are. It's a way of life. But it's mad when I think that I'm actually playing there nowadays and back then I used to skip away past bouncers. There would be ten of us and the minute the doors were opened it was like – bang! – and we were in and just all over the place, in all directions so that only some of us would get caught. I got thrown out a few times. We'd only go if it was something we enjoyed, that we liked.'

Stephen's life may have changed dramatically in the last five years, but the young superstar reveals that he still enjoys the simple pleasures of life such as reading books. 'I love sitting down, especially during the summer, and reading a book, its just so lovely. I read a lot. It's my favourite pastime. I read very spiritual books, like I'm reading a book called *Chicken Soup For The Soul*. It's a hundred and one short stories, telling you not to worry, life is too short, you've got to get on with your life. Don't worry till it happens. There are lots of true stories about people and after reading them you get a really good feeling. It cleanses your soul. It teaches you that whatever happens you've got to deal with it because our life is quick. I like reading those books...they make me smile and they make me feel more content. They teach you that you get back out of life what you put into it. I believe that.'

One of his greatest thrills nowadays is driving his new Peugeot 306 GTi. 'I was the only member of Boyzone who didn't have a car because I couldn't drive, so now I've learned how to handle one and it's brilliant. Peugeot gave me this car and I enjoy it, they put a CD player in it for me and they even put a kit in it for my phone. It's a lovely car, a lovely gold colour. My brother-in-law drove it and he said it's so smooth compared to his car, so he's jealous.

'All the other lads in Boyzone were totally mad into cars and I used to have to listen to them going on about "this engine and that engine" and I hadn't a clue what they were on about and it bored me. But now I'm interested and I quite enjoy those conversations. Of all the lads, mine is the only one that has a sixth gear, so they're jealous of that. When I was learning the instructor brought me all over the mountain and back down again. When we were up there I was terrified. It was nice and sunny down below but when we got up to the top it started to hail and then it started to snow. It was like blizzard snow. I haven't seen snow like that in Ireland in years, coming down really heavy. He said this was the test. I was going about five miles an hour. We did skid over a patch of ice but I didn't know what it was. I thought it was just snow but it was actually ice and I skidded. I was fine, clutch and brake. He said after that, "You're able to drive now. If you got through that you'd get through anything."'

When he's not working with Boyzone, Steve enjoys chilling out at home in Dublin. He says, 'I like to sleep, and do nothing, watch a bit of telly and catch up on the news. I love *Sky News*, I'm always watching *Sky News* on the hour, every hour. I just like to relax because it's my time. Sometimes I try and get acupuncture done if I'm really tired. They stick the pins in me and twist them. It's great, it gives you a whole buzz of energy. I like looking after myself. I do things that I want to do and if I have to do a lot during the day, running in and out of town doing bits and pieces, I like that as well because it's my time.

"I'm left alone most of the time when I'm out and about in Dublin. Generally girls meet you and they just say "How are ya, Stephen?" and they respect you. In all the interviews we have done, we say that our fans do respect us and if you need time they give you that space and it's true, they do. If I'm walking down the street in town or going for something to eat or drink or else just going to buy something in town, clothes or stuff like that, it's just "Hi!" and they're no problem, that's nice. We don't get hassle off the young ones, it's mostly the older people who give us hassle.

'When I'm in Dublin I usually hang out in hotels. I never go clubbing, I never go anywhere like that. There are too many people. You couldn't be doing with the hassle that you get from people my age or even older. There's no need for it, I don't want it. So why should I?'

Stephen also enjoys spending time with his little nephews, Jordan (his godchild) and Brendan, and he showers them with gifts. He says, 'Most of the time I spend down with Jordan and Brendan. I spend a lot of time with them because I want them to know who I am. I love my time with them. It's family stuff and I love all that. I'm Jordan's godfather. I buy them things, but I don't really spoil them. They're both only two, so they're not really conscious of what I do, although they see me on television. They are good kids and I love them. At the end of the day, it's people who are more important to me than anything I do.'

birthday boy

it was the glitziest Irish showbiz party of 1998 as Ronan's family and friends and fellow band members joined forces with stars from the worlds of showbiz, radio, TV and sport on Tuesday, March 3, 1998, to give the Boy a twenty-first birthday bash he'll never forget.

As his native Dublin played host to the biggest birthday party Ireland's capital city has ever seen, the entire country marvelled at how much this young man had achieved on a worldwide scale at such a young age.

'Superstar' is a term that doesn't sit easily on Ronan's young shoulders. He doesn't dwell on his celebrity status for fear of losing touch with reality. But he was accorded superstar treatment by the media during his birthday celebrations.

Ronan was front-page news for a couple of days and the country's national pop station, 2FM Radio, devoted an entire afternoon show to the affable Boyzone lad.

Even Ireland's monsters of rock U2 took time out from touring in Japan to personally phone Ronan at his country retreat. Bono's daughters are huge fans of Ronan and the Boyz and the U2 singer has been very supportive of Boyzone.

Ronan was thrilled when he received a personal birthday card from his heroes. But when he later heard their drummer Larry Mullen at the end of a phone line he was gobsmacked.

The day began for Ronan with a shopping trip into the city before heading back to his mansion where his Irish radio star pal Tony Fenton, a disc jockey with 2FM, was gearing up to present the birthday special.

Ronan grew up listening to Tony on the radio, not realising that one day the two would become good mates through their mutual love of music, radio and motorbikes. The Boyzone star enjoys working as a DJ and often drops in to co-present Tony's show in the Dublin studio.

"Why don't we do it from your bedroom and give away your duvet?"

Tony revealed; 'I got to know Boyzone when they first started. I listened to their first single, "Working My Way Back To You", and played it on my radio show, *The Hot Line*. Afterwards, they rang to say, "Thanks for the play." Then they invited me to see their video for "Love Me For A Reason". We had lunch and it was just like normal blokes having a chat.

'After that, anytime we'd meet up Ronan and I would always spend some time having a chat. He'd ring me and say, "Thanks for the play", or I'd ring him and say, "Do you want to come in to the studio?" Sometimes he'd come in just to say hello and we'd go for a beer afterwards.

'When I did my last *Hot Line* show before moving to a new afternoon *3 To 5 Live* programme, Ronan came in and co-presented it with me. I had a Harley Davidson motorbike and I brought him out for a spin on it a few times between soundchecks when they were playing in Dublin. I was always encouraging him to get one. Finally, he rang me and said, "I just got one today" and we spent the afternoon on the bikes. So a real friendship has built up.

'He'd drop into the studio when I'm on the air and sometimes he'd be sitting there having a coffee and I wouldn't mention that he's there if he didn't want people to know he was around. Last year he said, "I'd love to do the programme with you over Christmas, the whole week." But it didn't work out.

'I was over at his house during Christmas and he said, "I love doing the radio. I enjoy going on with you. Let's do something different the next time." So I said, "When is the next occasion? Your twenty-first is coming up shortly. Let's do something mad for that." He was going, "OK, let's do it from my house." I said, "Why don't we do it from your bedroom and give away your duvet." And that's how it happened.'

Tony had told the listeners that the March 3 show was being broadcast from a secret location and when Ronan let the secret out of the bag – that it was actually his country house – it didn't take long for a couple of hundred fans to turn up at the driveway to the sumptuous pad.

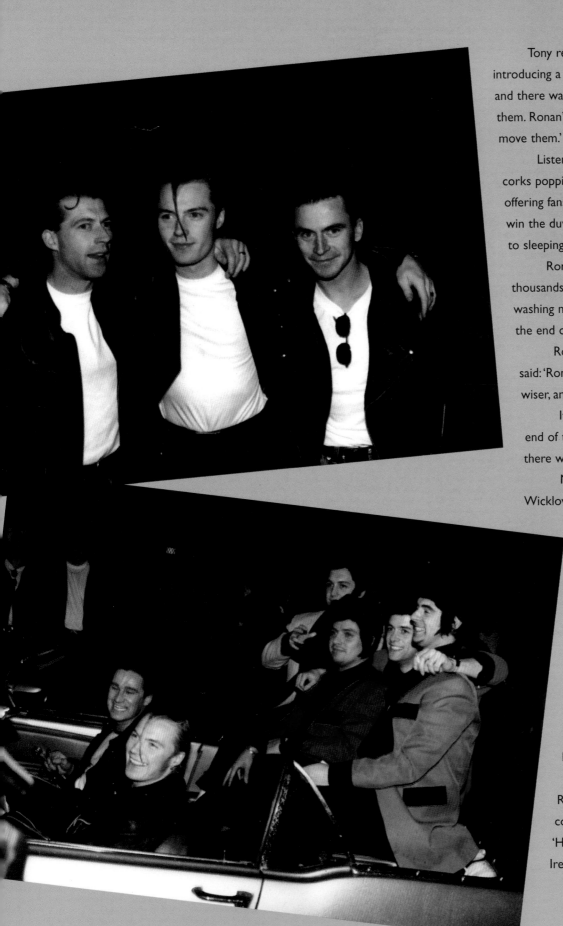

Tony revealed, 'I had just finished playing a record and introducing a record and I happened to glance out the window and there was all these kids on the driveway. Hundreds of them. Ronan's brothers and cousins had to go out and move them.'

Listeners to the show heard the sound of champagne corks popping as Tony and Ronan got into party mode, offering fans some special giveaways, including the chance to win the duvet off Ronan's very own bed, the next best thing to sleeping with the Boy himself.

Ronan selected dozens of birthday cards from the thousands that were sent to him. They were placed in his washing machine, given a spin and one was selected before the end of the show.

Ronan read out the message on the winning card. It said: 'Ronan Keating, another year older, another year wiser, another year sexier and more gorgeous to me.'

It suddenly dawned on the young girl at the other end of the phone line that she was the lucky person and there were gasps of 'Oh my God! Oh my God!'

Maria Nolan, aged fourteen, from Arklow, Co Wicklow, now has a Boyzone treasure that fans would die for. 'I'm going to put it on my bed and I'm going to sleep with it every night,' she told Ronan live on air.

The young schoolgirl admitted that not everyone shared her love of the band. 'I get teased for liking Boyzone, but no one is going to tease me now,' she laughed.

Maria wasn't the only caller to the show that day. World snooker champion Ken Doherty, who comes from Ronan's hometown, also phoned to wish the Boyzone star a happy birthday.

Local hero Ken dished out the plaudits to Ronan. 'I'd just like to say, Happy Birthday and continued success to Ronan,' he told the listeners. 'He's been fantastic as, indeed, have Boyzone for Ireland and for themselves. They are a credit to themselves and their country. You deserve everything you get, Ronan. Keep it up.'

As Tony played Ronan's favourite song of that moment, Allure's 'All Cried Out', the Boy sent out a special message to his lorry-driver dad Gerry over the airwaves. 'Get home, Da, we're waiting to blow out the candles.'

Ronan's joy was tinged with sadness on the day because his mum Marie had died just a month earlier. He had a special dedication on the show that day. It was R Kelly's massive hit, 'I Believe I Can Fly'. Ronan told the listeners, 'It was one of Mam's favourite songs. It's a beautiful record. It means a lot to me and all of the family.'

There were stacks of birthday cards all over the place and several birthday cakes presented to him by the media. The family dogs slipped into the house during the radio show and devoured one of the cakes which had earlier been presented to Ronan by a showbiz reporter from one of the daily tabloids.

The radio show had been a taster for the celebrations that followed later that night at trendy Dublin club, Red Box, owned by John Reynolds, one of Boyzone's managers.

Its location had been kept a closely guarded secret and there were only a handful of fans waiting outside when Ronan and his entourage arrived for the mammoth bash.

Inside, guests were transported back in time as the organisers tried to capture the atmosphere of the 1950s, with party-goers turning up in Teddy Boy outfits and the movie *Grease* playing in the background.

Ronan made a dramatic entrance, zooming in on his massive Harley Davidson motorbike with his girlfriend Yvonne Connolly on the back, in the style of John Travolta and Olivia Newton-John. It was the night the Boyzone star first proudly showed off his new love.

A fantastic classic Ford Mustang car was parked on the dance floor – a present from Shane, Steve and Keith. Car fanatic Ronan couldn't believe his eyes. It was a stunning gift from his Boyzone mates and it took his breath away. Ronan's little nephews, Conall and Ruairi, thought it was dead exciting too and spent the night hopping in and out of it.

Mikey and Keith arrived dressed in the Teddy Boy gear with their respective partners, Sharon and Lisa. Shane and Steve were also among the hundreds of people at the exclusive party, but they opted not to don the fancy dress. 'I got dressed up, but then chickened out,' Steve revealed.

Later in the evening, Keith slipped away to be transformed into a woman. He arrived out on stage to howls of laugher dressed to kill in a large blonde wig, a slinky gold lamé dress and a black feather boa. Along with his 'female' partner, disc jockey BP Fallon, Keith romped through a *This Is Your Life*-style sketch featuring some of Ronan's embarrassing moments.

Like the time he was given a week's suspension from primary school for fighting with the local bully. Like the time he accidentally hit his father under the eye with a golf club on a family holiday, resulting in Dad receiving several stitches. Like the time he hacked a chunk out of his hair with a pair of scissors, then covered the bald spot with a plaster to pretend he had a cut. Like the time the back of his pants ripped while he was serving a customer when he worked in a shoe shop.

There was also a pre-Boyzone video of Ronan from 1990 when he was captured in action playing football with his team Dunshaughlin.

Among the glitterati enjoying the festivities was the entire Newcastle United soccer squad, including Alan Shearer and John Barnes. But this was also a special family occasion and the entire Keating family were surrounded by their relatives and friends during the joyous occasion.

Dad Gerry, sister Linda, brothers Ciaran, Gerard and Gary and girlfriend Yvonne joined Ronan on stage as he blew out the candles on his birthday cake.

As Ronan thanked everyone for making his night so special, his voice cracked when he added, 'I wish my mother could have been here tonight...more than anything in the world.'

the contours of the jet-black Corvette car appear around the corner of a suburban roadway on the northside of Dublin city. Behind the wheel is a familiar, long-haired young man with a cheeky white smile that lights up the interior of his American automobile.

The motor is out of character in the neighbourhood where Keith Duffy grew up, but is in keeping with his image as a car fanatic. Like most young blokes, the dream machine is one of the joys of his life and the success of Boyzone has allowed him to indulge his passion for fast cars.

As Keith zooms up to his old school, Ard Scoil Ris on Griffith Avenue, he allows himself a wry laugh. His days there as a youth weren't happy ones and he certainly wouldn't like to turn back the years. Back then, he never dreamed that in a few years he would be a megastar who's idolised by girls all over the world.

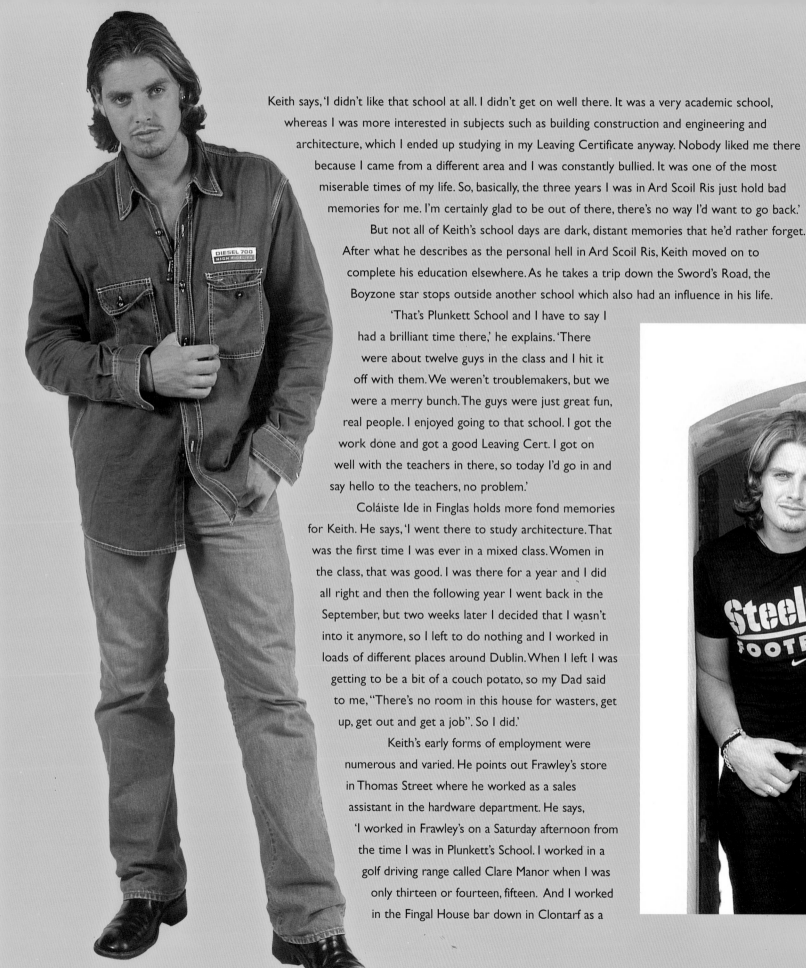

Keith says, 'I didn't like that school at all. I didn't get on well there. It was a very academic school, whereas I was more interested in subjects such as building construction and engineering and architecture, which I ended up studying in my Leaving Certificate anyway. Nobody liked me there because I came from a different area and I was constantly bullied. It was one of the most miserable times of my life. So, basically, the three years I was in Ard Scoil Ris just hold bad memories for me. I'm certainly glad to be out of there, there's no way I'd want to go back.'

But not all of Keith's school days are dark, distant memories that he'd rather forget. After what he describes as the personal hell in Ard Scoil Ris, Keith moved on to complete his education elsewhere. As he takes a trip down the Sword's Road, the Boyzone star stops outside another school which also had an influence in his life.

'That's Plunkett School and I have to say I had a brilliant time there,' he explains. 'There were about twelve guys in the class and I hit it off with them. We weren't troublemakers, but we were a merry bunch. The guys were just great fun, real people. I enjoyed going to that school. I got the work done and got a good Leaving Cert. I got on well with the teachers in there, so today I'd go in and say hello to the teachers, no problem.'

Coláiste Ide in Finglas holds more fond memories for Keith. He says, 'I went there to study architecture. That was the first time I was ever in a mixed class. Women in the class, that was good. I was there for a year and I did all right and then the following year I went back in the September, but two weeks later I decided that I wasn't into it anymore, so I left to do nothing and I worked in loads of different places around Dublin. When I left I was getting to be a bit of a couch potato, so my Dad said to me, "There's no room in this house for wasters, get up, get out and get a job". So I did.'

Keith's early forms of employment were numerous and varied. He points out Frawley's store in Thomas Street where he worked as a sales assistant in the hardware department. He says, 'I worked in Frawley's on a Saturday afternoon from the time I was in Plunkett's School. I worked in a golf driving range called Clare Manor when I was only thirteen or fourteen, fifteen. And I worked in the Fingal House bar down in Clontarf as a

lounge boy and a barman. It's gone now, it's changed its name. I worked in Dunne's Stores supermarket in Donaghmede Shopping Centre packing shelves, and I worked in Makullas clothes shop.'

Whenever Boyzone perform in Dublin's Point Depot, it revives memories for Keith of his time working there as part of the venue's security team. 'Now I'm on the other side of the fence,' he laughs. 'The Point has good memories for me. I started working there at a Metallica concert, doing front-stage security. I worked there for loads of concerts by performers like Peter Gabriel, Sinead O'Connor, Neil Young, Van Morrison and 4 Non Blondes.

'I had a very embarrassing incident during my time there. It happened after a Peter Gabriel concert and I was put on the Green Room door for the party afterwards, and only people with a certain pass were allowed in after the show. Bono and U2 were among the guests and when they walked past I was bit starstruck and I didn't stop them at all, and then the next guy to walk in was Johnny Depp and I stopped him for a pass because I didn't recognise who he really was.'

Returning to the days of his youth, Keith tells you about his sporting skills and how he played Gaelic football and hurling with his club Trinity Gaels. 'There is no actual clubhouse to mark those days, but I played for them from the time I was six years of age. I was six or seven when I first started playing for the Under-nines and I was with them right up to the Under-twenty-ones. So I was playing with them for a good ten or eleven years. I loved those games. I wasn't the best player, but I was one of the best. I played midfield in football and right-hand forward in hurling. And I loved both games, great fun, but when I started working on a Saturday I couldn't play Under-twenty one football. And then the band took off so I had to give it all up. Nowadays if I tried to play those games I'd probably get bashed.'

When the curtain comes down on the Boyzone roadshow and the Boyz return to their normal lives, Keith can be found at home with the two loves of his life, his beautiful wife Lisa who he married in Las Vegas in June and their cute young son, Jordan. Watching him acting the clown with Jordan, it's obvious that the child is the centre of Keith's universe. He admits that the pain of being separated from his son when he goes away for long periods working with Boyzone is often unbearable. 'Jordan and Lisa are very important to me, they are seriously important to me,' he says. 'I had loads of time with Jordan during the early part of this year which was fantastic and I was devastated when I had to go away. I'd become so used to being there that I'd forgotten what it was like to be away from them for so long. I was gutted and upset over it. I see them as much as I can.'

Returning home after touring with Boyzone has also brought problems for Keith and Lisa because of the difficulty of switching back from his role as a pop star to that of a husband and father to Lisa and Jordan. 'It takes most people a couple of days to settle down after they've been away for a fortnight's holidays. So you can imagine what it's like for me. I'm performing in front of thousands of fans who are screaming for us night after night, so it does take time to come down from that. I don't deny that myself and Lisa have had our problems as a result, but the test of our love is that we've always worked them out in the end and we're still together. Lisa and my mates and my family have just really stuck by me through all the madness that goes with Boyzone. They've kept me grounded. I don't think I've ever drifted in any way, but if I ever was to do that I would get a good clip on the ear from them and I'd be back to earth again. They're good for me,' he says.

As this book was being compiled, Keith and Lisa were living in a modest three-bedroomed semi-detached house in Dublin, although work has already begun on the building of their dream home. The magnificent five-bedroomed mansion has several stunning features, including a large conservatory at the back, a leisure room with a pool table and bar and a sauna and jacuzzi. It will be Keith's private castle to which he can retreat after his crazy life on the road.

There are more symbols of his amazing success outside his home, including a midnight blue convertible BMW, as well as a Corvette, which he bought from Boyzone's manager Louis Walsh. He also owns a Hummer, which looks like a tank, but it's a jeep

from the States. And then there's his Harley Davidson motorbike, which is a favourite 'toy' among the Boyzone group. Keith laughs as he shows off his impressive collection. 'One of these days I'll get the time to drive them all,' he says.

It's a balmy evening during early summer in Dublin and a group of young men are burning up energy as they engage in a fiercely competitive game of seven-a-side soccer on astroturf grounds in the northside area of Ballymun. There in the middle of them is one of pop's biggest stars, Keith Duffy, obviously relishing every moment of the match. It's this simple pleasure that means as much to Keith as all the trappings of his success.

Keith says, 'A friend of mine rang me up and said that he and all his mates from work were going to play a game of football and a couple of our mutual friends were going along as well. So I went down to watch and then they dragged me on to the pitch. There were gangs from all over the place playing there, loads of blokes and I was looking for trouble, really, because you can attract it in a situation like that. In the first few minutes I got a bit of stick, but after people realised that I was a young fella having a game of football, the same as everyone else, it was cool, it was grand. We played for hours and I had a great time. It was brilliant. They didn't understand how delighted I was to be invited.

'My friends are very important to me, the friends that have been there since I was fifteen or sixteen. They are my best buddies now and they're not taken away by this band thing at all. I can take friends of mine in the pop business that people look upon as huge stars and bring them out in Dublin with my mates and I know my mates aren't going to be starstruck. They get on great with them. They are really, really good mates, they've kept me together.'

Keith doesn't allow his star status to dictate the way he leads his life away from the stage. There are no burly bodyguards hovering around him and no chauffeur-driven limousines when he's out and about in his home town. 'If you're taken away by any of this fame at all, then you'll end up restricting the way you lead your life. You'd get to the stage where you wouldn't be able to go out shopping unless you had security and if you surround yourself with guys in dark suits and shades that only creates a crowd and a lot of hassle, so I just do my own thing.

'I walk down Grafton Street with Jordan, shopping, doing my own thing and it's grand. I sometimes get a little bit of hassle, but by the time people realise who you are, you are gone. They might look twice and the second time they look they might cop who you are. You might hear in the distance "That's your man from Boyzone" or "That's Keith Duffy". That's the way I do it...baseball cap, pair of shades...grand, no problem at all. I never have any problems.

'There are a certain few pubs and nightclubs obviously that I stay away from because, let's face it, there are a lot of childish people in the world. I could go into a pub. You get blokes after a few gargles [drinks] and they say things like "There's that prat from Boyzone", or whatever name they call you. I can ignore that to a certain extent, but I wouldn't trust myself after a few drinks. I wouldn't react nine times out of ten, but in case it's the one time out of ten, I refrain from going anywhere near those places.'

Keith enjoys returning to his home area whenever his hectic schedule allows him the time to relax and catch up on family life. His neighbours are proud of his achievements and today he welcomes their compliments. During the early stages of Boyzone, he admits he was a reluctant star. 'Initially, for the first couple of years, I didn't understand what was going on. I suppose out of embarrassment, in a shy kind of way I would keep my head down if I was passing anybody. It wasn't that I was rude or ignorant. It was a shy type of reaction. Nowadays I stop to say "Hello" and chat with the old ones on the road or kick football on the street with the lads, or whatever. I'm proud of where I come from and I love going back home.'

boyz in america

america – the land of Liberty where millions of Boyzone's Irish ancestors have emigrated for decades in search of a dream life. Cast a dime in the States today and you're sure to hit someone with an Irish background.

Boyzone are now hoping to make an impact on that vast territory, having already conquered Europe and the Far East. Stephen says, 'I love the States. We don't go enough. Louis, our manager, says we're really going to concentrate on the States in the New Year. I'm glad because I love the States, it's a brilliant place.'

The Boyz realise it's going to be a long, hard battle that will involve spending several months there and they're building up to 1999 when it will become their top priority. The seeds have already been sown, particularly during their whistle-stop tour of twelve States in July of 1997 and more promotion there this year.

Ronan says, 'It's really difficult to make it big in America because it's such a massive place. Each State is like a different country. But we're working hard on making Boyzone a household name there. It would be the icing on the cake for us.

'I think it's definitely a step Boyzone are going to take in the near future. We are all looking forward to it. We've worked everywhere else in the world, why not do it in the States. We are going to spend a couple of months out there. Give it a good shot.'

The Fab Five had lots of fun along the way last year as they jetted across South America and North America, dropping into cities en route to introduce themselves. Big is beautiful in America, so the Boyz weren't surprised to discover that their mode of transport during their brief sojourn in their first port of call, New York, was an ostentatious stretch limousine.

'I hate limousines,' Ronan says as it hovers into view. 'They're just so flash and it's not what we're into. They're so pretentious and they just attract attention.

'Obviously we do a lot of travelling and we like to have comfortable cars. I don't mind travelling in a Mercedes, but please don't give us limousines.'

Ronan and the Boyz just couldn't take themselves seriously as they stepped inside the big white limo on the mean streets of the Big Apple and snaps supremo Philip Ollerenshaw took lots of amusing photographs of them trying to look cool in the back of the massive car.

It was Keith's first time in New York and his jaw dropped as he scanned the massive skyscrapers. It was everything he thought it would be and more.

'I've seen this in films, but it's even bigger in reality,' he says. 'The traffic, the noise and the hustle and bustle is a great buzz. There's a tremendous energy here and it just sweeps you along, particularly when you come from a laid-back city like Dublin.'

Shane wasn't as enamoured because he likes a slower pace of life. 'It would be great if Boyzone made it big here, but it's all a bit too fast for me,' he sighed.

Although the Boyz didn't have a lot of free time to spare during their short visit to the Big Apple, a major effort was undertaken to show Keith the sights. Mikey has a sister who works in a bar on First Avenue, so he took Keith along to pay her a visit and pass on all the family news and gossip. Ronan also got the chance to hang out with his brothers Gary and Gerard who were there at the time. The Boyz also went to see the blockbuster movie *Men In Black*, long before it hit Europe.

Stephen said, 'I love New York. It's great. The other night we were in Central Park and it was pretty late. I was with Ronan and he said to me "Watch this", and he threw something at a bush. Suddenly you could see these fireflies – and I've never seen fireflies before – glowing all over the place in the darkness. It was amazing. I just wanted to catch them and bring them home. It was great. I've never seen that before and that was something really different.'

Shopping was also top of their agenda, as it is wherever the Boyz go, so they all headed off to the enormous Nike store. Stephen sneaked off and ended up in the Disney Store on Fifth Avenue! He was like a kid on Christmas morning as he browsed through the goodies on display. He says, 'That was funny. I said I would be back in an hour. The others couldn't find me. They were going "Where's Stephen?" Eventually I walked into our hotel with a Disney bag and they just looked at me and said, "Oh Jeez, we should have realised where you were going." I didn't want to bring them because the first time I went there with Shane and Ronan they did nothing but sit on the stairs and moan just because I went into the Disney store for ten minutes and they wanted to go into car shops. I just wanted to buy myself some Disney stuff. That's why I didn't bother asking them because I knew they'd say, "We're not going to a Disney store." The Disney Store over there has lots of stuff you can't get elsewhere. You can get lovely ornaments and get the proper cells from Pinnochio and all the animated films. They're very, very expensive. You can pay ten grand for a cell. You can spend a fortune on cells. I spent a bit, not that much, nowhere near ten grand.'

There was also work to be done on the trip and, as they did in every city they visited, Boyzone hosted a big press conference and met the fans at the local Hard Rock Cafe.

After a quick meal in New York's famous Benihana's, it was straight to the airport for a flight down to Puerto Rico where the Boyz got up to all kinds of wacky antics during a half day of free time.

Puerto Rico is in the Caribbean and it's one of the most gorgeous places on the planet. Taking advantage of the fantastic sunshine the Boyz wasted no time slipping into their bathing trunks and heading for the swimming pool. Several happy hours passed during which they chased each other in the

water, played basketball and held contests to see who could stay the longest in the freezing plunge pool and who could swim under the water for the greatest period of time.

The next morning it was back to business with a press conference in the local Hard Rock Cafe. Ronan said, 'The memorable thing about Puerto Rico is the brilliant time we had in the huge pool and in the sea and half a day to relax.'

Next stop was Miami for two days where Boyzone stayed at the Biltmore Hotel, which is one of the big grand hotels in a place called Corral Gables. The Biltmore is a real 1920s-style place with the largest swimming pool in North America.

Once again it was off with the gear and on with the togs as another swimming marathon kicked into gear. With the sun beaming down, the Boyz couldn't resist the opportunity to strive for a tan

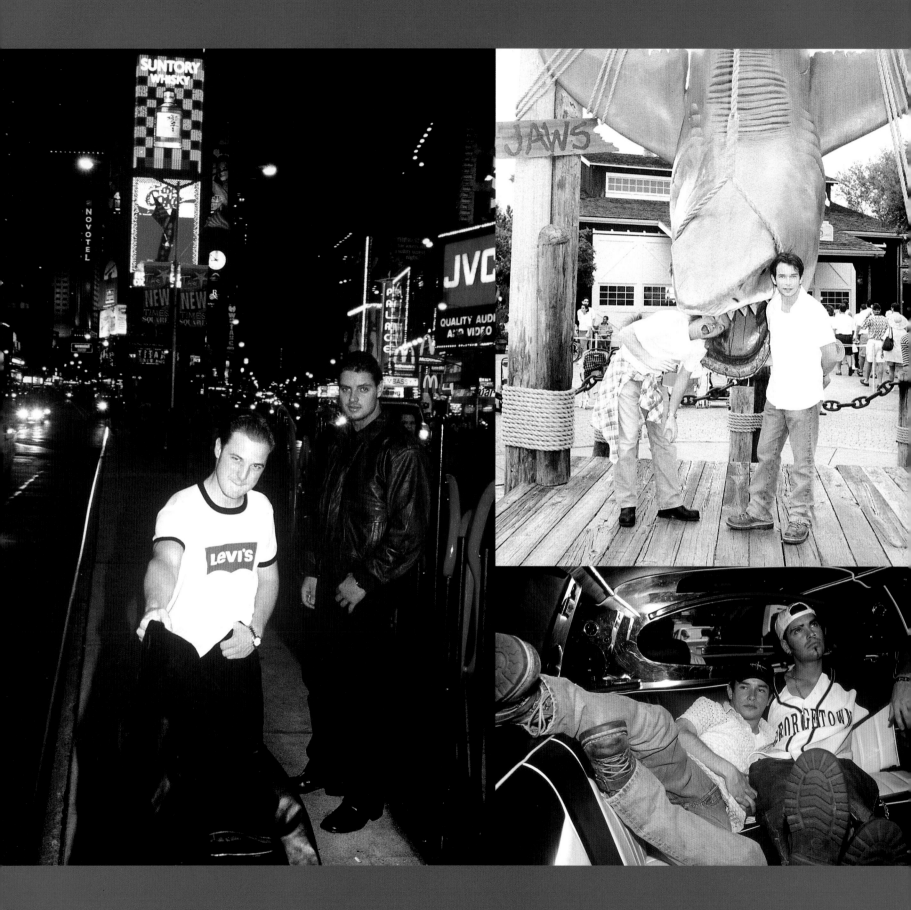

and Ronan managed to pack in too a round of golf on the magnificent course.

There were several photo sessions in the fabulous grounds of the breath-taking hotel, and all the interviews were conducted in Al Capone's suite, named after one of America's notorious gangsters from the 1920s. Apparently one of his bodyguards was murdered in the suite and you can still see the blood in the fireplace. It has been used in a lot of films, particularly the Will Smith movie, *Bad Boys*.

Stephen had a bizarre experience after Boyzone's stylist Alex injured himself and had to be carted off to hospital. He says, 'Alex was climbing on some mesh beside a pool to dive in and the fencing collapsed. He went down and a spike stuck into his foot. There was blood everywhere. The rest of the lads had to go and do interviews so I ended up sitting in a Miami hospital with Alex. It was like being part of the TV series *ER*, with all these Americans rushing around. Fortunately, Alex's injury wasn't serious. He got stitched up and all that. It was an experience being in the hospital.'

During their appearance at the Miami Hard Rock, Ronan met Chein Garcia, the composer of 'Mystical Experience', who had flown in specially from New Jersey to see the band in action and he revealed how he was very pleased with the Boyz' version of his song.

Then it was on to Orlando where the Boyz couldn't believe their good fortune after discovering that they were actually staying at the entrance to Universal Studios.

After their performance, Ronan, Stephen, Shane, Keith and Mikey headed straight for all the action in the pleasuredome. At the start, they were losing lots of time queuing for hours to check out Terminator 2 and all the different attractions until one of the staff, who happened to be Irish, spotted them and supplied them with a special pass which allowed them to jump the queues.

From then on it was plain sailing and they went on all the theme-park rides about three times, including Terminator 2, Back To The Future, Jaws, Earthquake and King Kong. It was virtual reality...King Kong attacks you in the cable car, that sort of thing. The newest one was Terminator 2, which was all in 3D and it was a mixture of live action and then 3D on the screen.

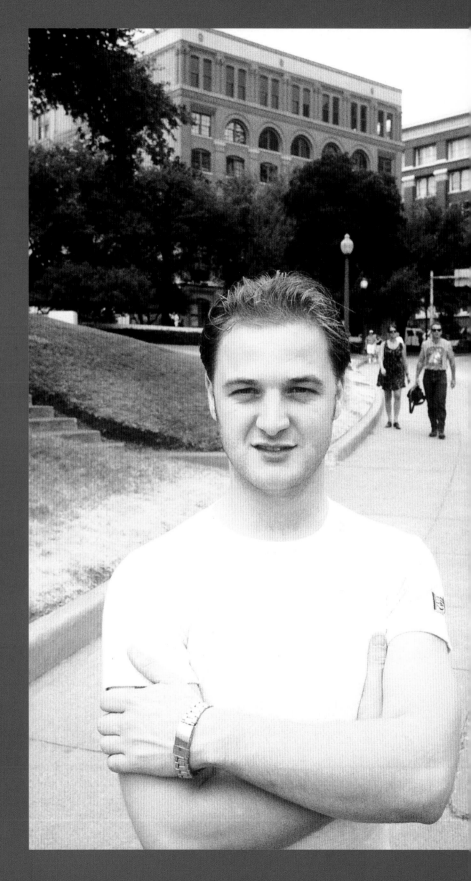

Then, on the way back to their hotel, the Boyz noticed three huge cranes with a big harness at the bottom; it was a bungee, but the other way around. Thrillseekers are strapped in a harness and then catapulted up in the air inbetween the three cranes and as you come down you swizzle round and round. Stephen went on it, as did tour manager Mark Plunkett, and Ronan and Keith. It turned out to be the highlight of the day.

Every morning the Boyz did a breakfast show. So it was Good Morning Texas, Good Morning Miami, Good Morning Dallas.

In Dallas one night the Boyz went out for dinner and took a ride by horse and cart from the restaurant back to the hotel. Stephen says, 'It was lovely, just going along the road, no cars, just this horse and cart which took about fifteen minutes. The guy was giving us a tour and you could see the window where President John F Kennedy was shot from. It was just bizarre because you see that in the films. I grew up watching the soap *Dallas* on TV and you see the buildings. You see all of them, they're all there. JR's offices, his buildings are all there.'

Keith says, 'It was total travel the whole time but I was just blown away with the States. In San Francisco, I actually met an ex-girlfriend from years ago and she was over there with one of my old best-mate's sister. They were there with a lot of girls who used to work with Lisa and they were all in the same gang. I was doing a gig in the Hard Rock in San Francisco in the evening time and I got a little piece of paper handed to me, like you do all the time. I don't know how but I managed to read this one. Not saying I throw my fan mail away or anything, but I actually managed to sit down and read this piece of paper and it was a phone number from this girl. I phoned her up and she came over to the hotel with all the girls, so we found the nearest Irish bar. We had the afternoon and evening off before flying to Los Angeles and we spent it in the Irish bar. I ended up drinking far too much and was in an awful state. Ronan was in a bad state as well at the end of it. He was so bad he got on the wrong flight. We were all in the airport looking for him and he was already halfway to Los Angeles after falling asleep and not realising he was the only member of Boyzone on the plane. That was funny. That's the way people over there actually expect us to be when they find out we're Irish, so on that occasion we lived up to our names.'

Then it was back to LA again to do a show and more interviews. One evening they headed off to Sunset Strip and checked out an Irish bar before going to the famous Viper Room nightclub.

Boyzone really had a good time in the States because they're completely unknown and it was only English and Irish holiday makers who recognised them in the theme-parks and stopped them for autographs and photos. There were also Irish and English fans at the Hard Rock Cafes after spotting posters saying 'Boyzone appearing here today' and hardly believing their eyes. It was the perfect chance for them to get close to the Boyz and it created a buzz for the press. It was a perfect venue because all the people could see Boyzone perform during the press promotion. They couldn't have done that in a hotel room or a function room in a hotel so the Hard Rock Cafe was a good place to stage their presentations.

Mikey says, 'The trip was a bit hectic and we were all very tired at the end of it. But I did enjoy it. I enjoyed everywhere, especially New York. I love New York. I like it because you can just walk down the street and nobody knows who you are. You can just be yourself, it's great. That's what I like about it.

'Both last year and again this year we have laid the foundation for us to get back and really concentrate on America in 1999. The guy who made Hanson big stars is going to look after us over there, so it all looks very positive. So in the New Year we will head over there for a couple of months solidly to break it.

'That's going to be the big one for next year. We are going to release an album over there, which will be a best of Boyzone-style album and hopefully it will go down well.'

'It was total travel the whole time but I was just blown away with the States.'

ron

1998 has been a landmark year in the personal world of Ronan Keating, one that will be indelibly etched in his mind for the rest of his existence on this earth. It's a year in which the young superstar has been confronted head on with the agony and ecstasy of life, forcing him to grapple with a whole range of emotions and events, from the grief and despair of losing his beloved mother Marie, to the joy and happiness of his surprise marriage to his Irish model girlfriend Yvonne. The manner in which Ronan has coped with his personal turmoil while sustaining a position as one of the pop world's most successful and busiest superstars has shown him to be a truly remarkable person.

Nowadays the Boyzone star lives his life in a constant whirlwind. And as he returns to the old haunts where he grew up, Ronan reflects on the simple life he enjoyed just a few short years ago.

The memories from those days are stirred as he gazes out at the little square in Bayside, on the northside of Dublin city, where he used to play football and hang out with the other kids. 'I spent most of my summer days over in that little square playing football, playing a game called tip the can and all those things. Everytime I drive past these days it brings back great memories from when I was growing up there with my family.'

The modest semi-detached house in an ordinary working-class housing estate of Bayside where Ronan lived with his parents, sister and three brothers, is still there. "It was a three-bedroomed house, but my Dad made it into four because there were so many of us. My memories from then are just of great years with all the family together. Nobody had gone to America then [his sister and brothers later emigrated to the States], we were all there. They were just great years.'

Bayside Youth Club was one of his regular hangouts just before he became a teenager. 'I used to go there at weekends, myself and Trev, my cousin, and my pals. It was the usual youth club, there were always games going on. Just a regular youth club on a Saturday night. I would have been ten or eleven at the time.'

Ronan and his family moved to the country in his early teenage years, setting up home in the rural community of Dunshaughlin, Co Meath. It was there in the local community college that he experienced the prejudices and problems of being a city kid in the country. He says, 'We moved down to Meath as my Mam opened a hair salon here. I was a Dublin boy in a country school. It didn't go down too well with the locals in the school. But I made a few good friends there who saw through all of that. There was Mark and Vinnie, Tommy and Matthew.

'Despite everything, standing outside the school today I can honestly say that I have very good memories of my time there. It was a lot of fun. I didn't get into the fights and brawls young fellows get into, especially when your a Dub [Dubliner] living in the country. I have very good memories. I rarely leave bad memories anywhere, I always try to make the best of everywhere.'

Dunshaughlin Athletics Club was also a major part of Ronan's early years. 'I was running for them when I was living in Dunshaughlin,' he says. 'I did extremely well, much better than I expected to, I won the National finals in the 800 metres and 200 metres. All my years while I was in Dunshaughlin I was in the Athletics Club.'

During his school years in Dunshaughlin, Ronan displayed signs of his talent as a singer when he fronted a local band and ended up winning a talent competition, scooping a whopping £1,000, which was a fortune to him at the time. 'The band was called Nameste and we used to jam together all the time and enter contests. It was really cool. I was always interested in music, ever since I was a kid. Myself and my brother Gary used to have all the latest albums and records.
I like to think that a career in music was always on the cards, but I didn't know it back then.'

Three years after they moved to the country, the Keating family were back living in Dublin and Ronan went to the St. Fintan's secondary school in Sutton, run by the Christian Brothers. 'I was there through fifth and sixth years and they were brilliant years,' he recalls. 'My cousin Trev and myself were there together. It was cool because he used to live right beside the school, so we used to go down to his house for lunch. Anytime I wanted to be on the hop [skipping school] I could always go down to Trev's house. Trev's always around me these days in Boyzone. He's a dear, dear friend of mine.

'When I was in my final year in school, along came the band. I worked in a Dublin shoe shop called Korky's for a long time as well, while I was still in my final years at St. Fintan's and just before Boyzone took off. I had four months left in school and up came Boyzone so I had to decide Boyzone or school and my Mam said it was up to me to make the choice. I think it was the right choice.'

The Ormond Centre in the city of Dublin is another building that figures in Ronan Keating's early life. 'It's where it all began five years ago,' he points out. The Ormond is the venue where Boyzone boss Louis Walsh held the auditions to form his supergroup.

Ronan recalls: 'I remember myself and my friend Mark Maher joined the queue and Mark was going to go for the audition as well. But when we got there he was like, "I won't, I won't", so he didn't bother. So there was just myself. I remember I was in the paper that day for Korky's. I had modelled some shoes and I came up with the paper clipping and gave it to Louis. It's funny now when I think about it. I had to sing 'Father And Son' because everybody had to sing it. I knew it, but I wasn't too confident about singing it because it was very high vocals. I turned to Louis and I said, "Do you mind if I sing another song?" Then I had to go and sing 'Careless Whisper' and everything went well. Then they asked us back for the second time, and then we had the third round and it was brilliant when I got in. It was an amazing few weeks. I'll never forget it. It was like the week I did the Eurovision.

'Looking back, it seems like an awful long time ago. I am twenty-one now and I was just gone fifteen when I joined the band and it seems like a very long time and we've learnt so much and have grown up so much in those years. It seems like a lot longer than it actually was. We've done so much, travelled the world, been through so much in our lives, the five of us.'

Boyzone exploded on to the scene achieving a level of success way beyond the hopes and aspirations of everyone involved in the group. It has made Ronan a household name and today he has all the trappings of a high-flier, including a beautiful home perched proudly in the picturesque Irish countryside.

The magnificent mansion also stands today as a monument to the wonderful relationship Ronan enjoyed with his beloved mother Marie. Ronan bought it as a family home near the scenic village of Straffan, Co Kildare, for his dear Mum just a few months before she died. She absolutely adored the place and it brought her so much joy and happiness during her final days on this earth.

'It has meant the world to me that I could do that for her,' Ronan says. 'Mum gave me everything I have and the only way I could give it back to her was through things like that.'

February 2, 1998, is a date that will be forever etched in Ronan's memory.

It was the day that the Boyzone star's whole glittering world came crashing down around him when his beloved mother Marie passed away in hospital at the age of fifty-one following a brave fight against cancer.

Ronan recalled how he had a strange premonition that his mother was going to leave him. 'The night before, I had dreamt in bed that my Mam had died and that she was sitting on a chair beside myself and my sister Linda, telling us, "I'm gone now. I've no more pain. Let me go." When I woke up I told everybody in the house and then we got the phone call.'

Marie's death brought shock, despair and unbearable heartache to all the Keating family. 'We never knew she was dying,' Ronan says. 'She'd had breast cancer and she got the all clear and it was celebration time. Then two weeks before Christmas we discovered there was a tumour at the top of her spine. We thought she would pull through, but sadly we were wrong.'

Ronan wasn't there in the final moments. 'If she didn't have her five children around her, she didn't want any of us to be there. That's the way my Mam was,' he says.

'Two of my brothers were in New York. My sister Linda who had come home from America and given up her whole life to look after Mam was there on the morning of February 2. Mam obviously knew her time was close and she sent Linda away to buy some slippers in the local shopping centre.

'When Linda was gone, Mam called the nurse. The nurse sat beside her. She told the nurse all about her five wonderful children...and then she passed away.'

For those who have lost loved ones, it's a sad reminder of the terrible anguish, pain, bewilderment and utter devastation that death brings.

It was a cruel blow to Ronan at a stage in his life where he had the world at his feet. In the immediate aftermath of his mum's passing, he was plunged into a state of total confusion. Marie had been the rock in his life, the centre of his universe. She was also his best friend. Ronan had phoned her every day, no matter where he was in the world. Ronan was her baby and she worried about him all the time. She was always encouraging him to look after his health and to get more sleep.

A pained expression breaks across Ronan Keating's face as he reflects on the loss of this very special lady who shaped him as a person and will continue to be an influence in his life.

'Words can't describe my Mam,' he says. 'She was the best in the world. She was there for all of us. She was such a strong woman and the most important thing to her was her family.

'She was very proud of what I achieved. She was very proud of all the family, my three brothers and sister Linda.'

He says he owes all his success to Marie and would happily give up all his fame and money and possessions to have her back. 'Mum supported me from the very beginning when I told her I wanted to leave school and concentrate on a career with Boyzone. She said, "It's up to you. Just promise me you'll go back to school if you fail." She backed me all the way and, fortunately, I made the right decision. I'm sure it was a great relief to her the way things worked out for Boyzone.'

The funeral service for Marie was a private family affair at their request, with just a few celebrity friends in attendance. Steve, Keith, Shane and Mikey were also there to support Ronan.

The fans stayed away to allow Ronan, his dad Gerry, sister, Linda and brothers Ciaran, Gerard and Gary to grieve away from the glare of prying eyes and he's very grateful to them for honouring his wishes.

It was a sad event, but there were moments when laughter filled the air in the church of Straffan village as Ciaran and Gerard recalled happy memories and expressions of their darling mother.

Ronan did one of the readings and it was probably the most difficult performance of his life. 'It's easy to do this in front of 20,000 people, but not in front of Mam,' he told the congregation as he glanced down at the coffin.

Singer Brian Kennedy sang 'Carrickfergus', one of Marie's favourite songs. And Irish performer Finbar Furey played the pipes at the graveside as Marie's remains were laid to rest.

Ronan immediately tried to pick up the pieces of his shattered life by plunging himself into a tough work regime with Boyzone. He also had the love and support of his family. 'I have a fantastic family. We all stuck together,' he says.

What they are left with are memories, wonderful memories of a kind and loving mother. 'She's still here,' Ronan says. 'She's getting me through this.'

Ronan says his mother will live on in his music and in him. He has written several songs about his mum on the new Boyzone album 'Where We Belong'. 'She will live forever in my heart and in my songs,' he says.

Three months later the Boyzone star was caught up in another momentous personal event – this time a deliriously happy one – when he stunned the pop world and Boyzone fans by secretly marrying his gorgeous girlfriend Yvonne Connolly on the Caribbean paradise isle of Nevis. Ronan says he never experienced such joy as he did the moment the couple exchanged their wedding vows on Thursday, May 7. He reveals: 'It was the happiest day of my life. It may have seemed like a surprise to some people, but I knew it was the right decision for me.'

The wedding took place at a time when some newspapers were reporting that Ronan had suffered a breakdown after pulling out of an appearance on Top Of The Pops to promote 'All That I Need'.

Ronan says 'I didn't have a breakdown at all. I was just tired. I was worn out and everything got built up inside my mind and heart. My mother's death hit me hard. I don't think I'll ever come to terms with it to be honest. I don't think you can, as much as people tell themselves they're fine and tell other people they're fine. I don't think I'll ever come to terms with that, but I do realise now what has happened and that was the hardest step just realising.

'I just needed time away from all the madness. One of the steps was marrying Yvonne...the next step in my life was to do that. It was something we talked about for a long, long time and we had plans. And it's something we both wanted together. So we did it.

'We'd known each other for a long time and we were best friends. The next step from that was to walk away and I couldn't because I was crazy about her. I was afraid if I told her how I felt that she wouldn't feel the same and that it would break my heart. So I thought the best thing for me was to walk away, but I got Dutch courage one night and decided to tell her how I actually felt and she said she felt the same, so the rest is history as they say. We've been together ever since and we're happy. I've never been as happy in my life.

'I proposed to her before we went away. It was very romantic and beautiful...very special for both of us and something we will remember for the rest of our lives. I went down on one knee, the whole lot.

'I first met Yvonne when was about thirteen or fourteen years of age. My Dad used to deliver minerals around Ireland and there was this shop next door to Yvonne and I went in one day and she was there and she said "Hello." Nothing happened and I went away. I got sick the next week, so I never went back. She went back the next week and my Dad was there and she asked, "Where's Ronan?" and my Dad told her I wasn't coming back because I was sick. So I never saw her again until just a bit before last year's Eurovision.

'Yvonne has been a tower of strength to me since Mam died. She has been there for me through it all. She has been my best friend. I don't know what I would have done without her and without my family. Everybody...Ciaran, Linda, Gerard, Gary...we are a tight family and we all stick together. And now that I'm with Yvonne we'll tackle anything together the two us, and we'll stand tall.

'The response we've got from all our friends and from all of the people around us has been, "Congratulations and fair play to you, we're over the moon with happiness for you", and that's all we want to hear at the end of the day.

'I have to say the reaction of the fans has been brilliant as well. They have been very mature about it. We're really happy about that. I was worried about the fans' feelings.. how it would be. They've been so supportive of both of us. When Yvonne goes around Dublin on her own and they see her, they say "Yvonne, fair play". They have been brilliant. I expected they'd be upset which would be understandable, but they've all been brilliant.'

The newly weds now live in Ronan's six-bedroomed home, along with his dad Gerry and sister Linda. Ronan says, 'We love it there. It's beautiful and peaceful. I have a studio down the back. I've built it up and up and it's a good recording studio now. The house also has an amazing sitting room in it. It's the biggest room in the house and it's probably the most peaceful. There's a big open fire and you can just sit there and watch TV or just read. It's such a wonderful room.

'I have all the cars and bikes there. I have the Ford Mustang that Steve, Shane and Keith bought for me. I have a Ford Bronco which is an American truck. My favourite car is, of course, my Peugeot 406. I drive that all the time. It's a wonderful car. Drive that all the time. I also have Volkswagen Polo, and several motorbikes, including a Harley Davidson. Sadly, I don't have much time to enjoy them all, but I know there will be a time when I can.

'Playing golf is also one of my passions now. I play down in the K Club, which is near where I live. People are very good to me down there and it's nice and quiet. I go down there with Yvonne's father, her brother, with my brother Gary or Ciaran. There's always someone to play golf with. I know the Irish champion Christy O'Connor Jnr very well. He gave me a few lessons and we had a laugh. And I was out with Colm Montgomery. I'm not great at golf and I'm not intimidated playing with people of that calibre. I just tell them how I am and they give me tips. You've got to start somewhere.'

eastern world

i t's March 1998 and both Ronan and Stephen are in Japan where they're
promoting the Boyzone single 'Picture Of You' and attending premieres of the
Mr Bean movie, as this is the last territory where it has been released.

Japan is one of the most fascinating countries the Boyz have
encountered during their globe-trotting experiences and they're
delighted to be back, although it's a strange feeling to be talking about
'Picture Of You' and *Bean* nine months after its release back home.

Stephen had gone to Japan ahead of Ronan who stayed behind
in Ireland for the final of Eurosong 1998, Ireland's national contest to
find a song to represent the country in the Eurovision Song Contest.
Ro had written a song called 'Make The Change' for his pals the Carter
Twins, but unfortunately it wasn't chosen.

Meanwhile Steve was working around the Japanese cities of
Tokyo, Sapporo, Hakata, Fukuoka and Oida. He says, 'I was in Japan for
five days before Ronan joined me. The day before Ronan arrived I had
to do fourteen interviews by myself. That was my toughest day.'

Like most trips involving promotion, there's a lot of whizzing
around the place. But instead of travelling in the comfort of
chauffeur-driven cars, Ronan and Steve take the 'bullet' trains
along with the locals.

With Japanese cities being so densely populated – it's the eighth
largest country in the world with a population of around 126 million –
trains are the most efficient way of getting around.

The sight of Ronan and Steve hauling their suitcases through
train stations with lots of Japanese fans hovering in the background
was a daily occurrence.

Photographer Phil Ollerenshaw wasn't at all happy about being forced to lug his suitcases to the trains. 'I was whingeing like mad,' Phil admits. 'But there wasn't a word from Ronan and Stephen. They never even thought about it. To them it's getting from A to B...carry your own suitcase...you don't have someone carry it for you.

'Boyzone have always fought against that. They're not into the big limousines and they don't like to be surrounded by bodyguards and people who look after their every whim. They like to be normal lads doing a job. They are very like that.

'It was all fun. The Boyz had twenty or thirty fans running after them everywhere they went. It was a different way of doing a promotion trip. It was like being on holiday.

'But the place really is milling with people. When you arrive at the train station there are 500 taxis outside. That is no exaggeration, the whole place is clogged up with taxis and people. The stations are incredible. There are forty platforms. You have to book a seat on the train. It's just like going on a plane.'

There are many reasons why the Boyz love Japan...two of them are shopping and food. Every spare hour in their manic itinerary usually involves a mad dash to the stores. And this trip was no exception.

Ronan and Steve discovered that there's a new product in Japan called a DVD, which is going to take over from videos. It's a Digital Video Disc, which is about twice the size of a CD walkman and it plays films. The top flips up, you slip in your disk and there's a little screen so that you can watch it on planes or you can plug it into your TV at home and have perfect digital quality.

Ronan and Steve were determined to get their hands on this latest gadget, so between every radio and TV interview they were dashing around to electrical stores in a mad search for the DVDs until they eventually found them.

Steve says, 'The picture is the best quality you could possibly imagine. Myself and Ronan treated ourselves to one and we bought about fifteen films each and mine included a load of Disney movies.

'We really enjoyed our adventure through the stores and they're all enormous. But instead of saying you have half a day to go shopping, we had half an hour here and there. So it's like when we were in New York, we crammed in as much as we could as there is so much to do and so much to see.

'In each major hotel where we stayed there were up to twelve restaurants underneath in the basement, along with a whole shopping complex. So it's not as if you're stuck in a boring hotel. If you have half an hour to spare between interviews you can dash down and buy something.'

Japan, which consists of a chain of islands, is a stunning place to see and travelling on the trains gave the Boyz the opportunity to catch a glimpse of several towns and cities that they would otherwise have missed out on.

Steve says, 'Supporo was an amazing place. Snow was falling and the ground was white...it was so like Christmas. People were skiing in the mountains and there was just a lovely atmosphere there.'

Sampling the local cuisine was also high on their list of priorities and Stephen and Ronan enjoyed all the local traditions.

Ronan explains, 'When you meet Japanese, it's polite to bow slightly from the waist and incline your head, although they don't expect foreigners to carry on like that. Nowadays many Japanese have taken to shaking hands, although the bow is still the most important mark of respect.

'You are also expected to sit on the floor with your legs underneath you when socialising with the Japanese or visiting them in their homes and after a long time this can be painful. But you have to be careful when stretching your legs so that you don't point your feet at people because this is considered bad manners.

'I'm told that it's not considered polite to use a handkerchief for blowing your nose in public there, so if you've got a cold the proper thing to do is to keep sniffing until you get to a private place to do your business.

'One of the best reasons for going to Japan is the food. It's certainly half the fun of being there. We have sampled some of Japan's better-known dishes at home, but they don't compare to the delicious offerings we got in the country itself.

'Japanese food is far more than just sushi, tempura and sukiyaki which is what it's known for at home. You could spend a month in Japan and sample a different speciality restaurant every night.

'The Japanese are also big into praising, so if you make the effort to learn a few sentences of Japanese or you use the chopsticks in restaurants, they really appreciate it and tell you so.'

You can't go anywhere in the world without bumping into the Irish and Osaka was no exception for Boyzone when they met their old pals Bono and the

boys from U2, who were playing there as part of their PopMart world tour, and it turned into a very long night at their hotel. 'It was all hours when we left their hotel, we had a great laugh,' Ronan says. 'They are the same as we are, no different. Just lovely, down to earth lads...salt of the earth.'

Ro and Steve also got a chance to spend some time chatting with a group of their Japanese fans who followed them everywhere on the trip.

Phil Ollerenshaw revealed, 'It was a lot more relaxed on this trip because there was just Ronan and Stephen, instead of all five Boyz together. So at night the two of them would go in the bar and there'd be about thirty fans there.'

Although the Japanese people tend to be quite shy, when you meet young people in bars they tend to be surprisingly forward in making contact, particularly after a few drinks. Generally all it takes is a smile and a nod to be brought into conversation.

Steve said, 'It was just a nice way of learning about people. A lot of these people have been fans for years and have known us for a long time. But it's just nice to get a chance to speak to some of the fans in a normal, relaxed atmosphere. And it was a conversation about life. It wasn't a conversation about Boyzone. It gave us a good insight into the local Japanese people.

'We saw the same thirty fans you see every day because they followed us everywhere, but they were very well behaved. I don't know if they are very wealthy or that this is just what they decide to spend their money on but they seemed to have lots of time and the expense of all the travelling and hotels didn't seem to be a problem. It's just a different way of life there.'

The exchange of gifts is also an important part of Japanese life. It needn't be anything big, but gifts are used for cementing friendships.

Ronan says, 'Each one of those thirty people gave us a really nice present because the Japanese culture is very giving orientated. That is the way you make your loved ones feel welcome. It's all the wrapping and the ceremony of the present to them that is important. You may receive this fantastic box with all this handmade paper and bows, beautifully wrapped and in it there may be a small piece of pottery which you don't really understand. But it may be something handmade by the fans or it may be a Calvin Klein jumper. But irrespective of what the present is, it's the presentation and the giving of the present that's so important to the Japanese.

'I'd say the fans were aged between sixteen and twenty-five. They weren't young girls...they were all the same fans we met the last time we were in Japan. We went bowling with them.'

'I decided to do something about my hair as it was sticky and uncomfortable'

Going on tour in Japan, the Boyz got the opportunity to visit a place called the Golden Temple in Kyoto where there are more than 2000 temples and shrines, a trio of palaces and dozens of gardens and museums. Kyoto is the old capital of Japan and the Boyz were there in the spring when it's really beautiful, even though it was pouring with rain.

After a traditional meal, Ronan and Stephen went to the temple and made offerings to the gods, made their wishes over burning incense and then sat down for the traditional cups of tea.

Mr Bean himself, Rowan Atkinson, had been in Japan the previous week promoting his film, so Stephen and Ronan had to attend the premières on their own. They covered seven different cities in ten days, making appearances at screenings of *Bean* and then doing questions and answers sessions on stage.

They also met fans who won competitions through local radio stations. It's all very different in Japan...instead of going up and having pictures signed, the Japanese all sit in the theatre and the Boyz go up and shake their hands.

There's no queuing for hours outside a record shop, squashed behind barriers. You walk into the room and all the fans are sitting on the floor being nice and polite. They put up their hands and ask questions.

One of the radio stations had a glass screen to the outside world so that the actual DJs can be seen by people walking past on the street. When Boyzone were there, hundreds of fans were all

trying to get a glimpse of their idols. Instead of them all being crushed, the security guards would let twenty girls pass at a time and they'd stand at a barrier and wave at Ronan and Steve before moving on. Everything is done very orderly and cleverly so that the fans get a chance to see things in a relaxed fashion.

Steve says, 'This was a great trip to Japan. I loved Tokyo. It's very like New York...a very hypnotic place. It's a place you get caught up in. My only regret is that I didn't get the chance to visit the Tokyo Disneyland but maybe next time.'

The summer of 1998 found the Boyz back in South East Asia promoting their new album *Where We Belong*. This trip followed their autumn 1997 live tour which saw Ronan, Stephen, Shane, Keith and Mikey create scenes of hysteria wherever they appeared.

Photographer Phil Ollerenshaw was on the tour and he recalled, 'The nice thing about that trip is that Boyzone had been to a lot of the places before, so when they weren't working there was a lot of lazing by the pool, going shopping and eating and drinking. But there was also a lot of travelling involving four-hour flights and seven-hour flights because Boyzone also performed in India and and the Middle East.'

In Bahrain, Shane got a hairstyle that the other Boyz later christened 'Pineapple Head'. He revealed, 'It was really hot in Bahrain, so I decided to do something about my hair as it was sticky and uncomfortable. We were on the beach and we met this little old lady who couldn't speak much English, but she offered to braid it. The braids only lasted for seven days, but I liked it so much I got it done professionally when I got home. The only trouble was, I couldn't walk down the street because everyone recognised me.'

Shane proudly unveiled his 'pineapple' hairstyle in the video for the Boyzone hit, 'Baby Can I Hold You', and on the opening of the Something Else tour. His selection of blue braids were created during a marathon four-hour session with the hairstylist!

Stephen says, 'Bahrain was my favourite place. It was just beautiful for me. I remember me and some of the lads out on the beach. The sea was blue and the sand was white, the hotel was just there and you walk out on to the sand. We hired out a boat, me, Ronan, Shane and Keith... Mikey stayed in bed as always! It was absolutely beautiful. We were going along in the boat, all lying down getting a bit of sun, and you could see these dolphins in the water, just jumping up all around you. You could put your hand in the water. I love the sea because me and the sea just have something. The lads were all there, the wind blowing in your face. Then the experience I had water-skiing...I had never done water-skiing before. And then I went para-gliding. I've always wanted to do para-gliding. I was up there, it was a dead breeze, I was gliding and the sun was shining on me. I said a prayer and thanked God for giving me the opportunity to be actually in Bahrain because none of this would have happened if the band hadn't happened. It was just lovely. Fifteen minutes up there and I came back down with a really good feeling.'

One of the highlights of Boyzone's rampage through South East Asia was their time in the tropical paradise of Bali. It's rich in culture and has beautiful landscapes and coastline. The Boyz fell in love with it. English is understood in all the tourist areas, violent crime is uncommon and there is no drug scene. The markets are like an Aladdin's cave, so again there was lots of shopping and Ronan picked up several ethnic ornamental things for his new home.

Philip says, 'The promoter in Bali put on a big show for the Boyz and gave them the superstar treatment. He had just built an incredible stadium by the sea, which he's turning into a theme park.

'He put the Boyz in the best hotel, which was a really stunning place, and he held a huge barbeque in their honour. All the lads wore the traditional saris, which is like a cotton skirt. There was lots of sunbathing and pina coladas by the pool, so it was really idyllic and a very memorable time for the guyz.'

the air is filled with the sounds of birds chirping, cows mooing, dogs barking and a happy little toddler playing with her latest Barney toy. It's a scene of domestic bliss in the lush countryside outside Dublin city, in stark contrast to the frenzy that surrounds Boyzone when they're touring.

Mikey Graham relaxes on a couch in the sitting room of his palatial six-bedroomed dormer-style bungalow, nestling among trees and green fields in farming country and reflects on his wacky double life.

This is Mikey's little piece of heaven, his own private haven a world away from the mayhem that goes with a career in the fast lane of pop. As he gazes out through the window of his sitting room to fields where cows are grazing peacefully 200 metres away, Mikey says, 'I find it very relaxing and therapeutic here.'

Wandering through the tastefully decorated homestead, Mikey proudly shows you his favourite room in the house. It has its own private bar and the centre piece of furniture is a pool table.

He says, 'I have a stereo system in here and I like to blast a few CDs now and then. It's my recreational room. Sometimes I have pals around and they stay the night. We shoot a bit of pool, have a drink or two and then start talking rubbish all night, thinking we're making loads of sense."

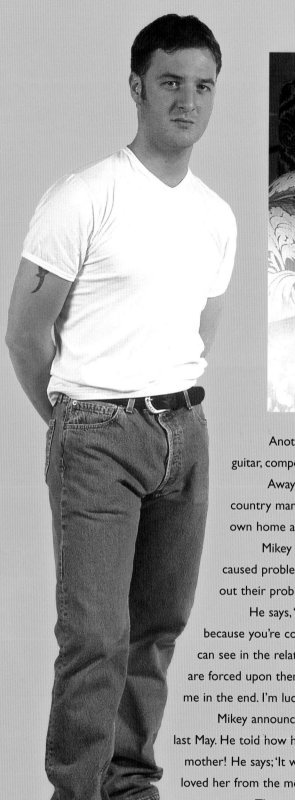

Another room has been converted into Mikey's personal music studio, where he plays his guitar, composes songs and builds up a repertoire of material that may one day surface after Boyzone.

Away from the stage, Mikey enjoys a normal family life these days. He shares his comfortable country mansion with his beautiful fiancée Sharon and their two-year old daughter Hannah. 'I've me own home and all that now and I'm pretty well settled,' he says.

Mikey readily admits that juggling a jet-set career while trying to hold down a relationship caused problems in his personal life and he and Sharon separated at one point. But they have worked out their problems and are now one of pop's happiest couples, blessed with a gorgeous little daughter.

He says, 'The pop lifestyle is hard for a partner or girlfriend or whatever to contend with because you're constantly away. The other half has to put up with an awful lot. Sometimes, as everybody can see in the relationships with people involved in showbiz, there are break-ups due to the pressures that are forced upon them by the whole situation. I've been through that, but thank God it has all worked out for me in the end. I'm lucky.'

Mikey announced his engagement to Sharon at the launch of their album, *Where We Belong*, in London last May. He told how he popped the question by giving their daughter Hannah an engagement ring for her mother! He says; 'It was a very special moment and a total surprise for Sharon. I've never felt happier. I've loved her from the moment I met her. I gave Hannah the ring and as she gave it to her mother I popped the question. There were tears and laughter when she said, "Yes!" – we were both in shock. I am going to marry the mother of my child and it's the best feeling in the world. I love this woman to bits.'

When he's not hitting the Boyzone trail, Mikey spends the time in his home and says he has become very domesticated. 'Yes, that's what I do now. But it's a bugger looking after the house,' he

laughs. 'Because I live out in the countryside, it's very hard to get a cleaner to travel this far, so you've got to do it all yourself. I'm quite good at household chores. I have me days.

'I do a bit of cleaning. From Monday to Saturday I throw all my clothes on the ground and then Sunday, at least one day a week, I pick them all up. I'm not bad at cooking either, but it takes a lot of encouragement to get me in to do it. It's not one of my specialities. I am very handy around the house, doing things like sticking up pictures and fixing things. I always was like that, even when I lived with my mother. From the age of thirteen, fourteen or fifteen I took over from my father doing all the wall papering and painting and all that kind of stuff around the house. I just got great enjoyment out of doing it. I'm sure my parents were delighted that they had a young lad who did a good job of it all.'

One of the prettiest rooms in the spacious house is Hannah's. It's got pink walls and pink carpets and Barney items are everywhere. There is also a big bouncy castle which Mikey bought her for her second birthday on May 1, along with an impressive Barbie electric jeep.

'Hannah loves it,' Mikey says as he gazes lovingly at the little girl. 'She likes sitting in it, but is afraid to press the pedal to go in it. She is a bit young for it, so Sharon sits in it with her

on her lap and it drives the two of them around. It's great, although it drives me around the bend!'

It's so obvious watching Mikey lost in a different world as he plays with Hannah that he adores his young daughter. 'Oh yes, absolutely,' he says. 'She's two now and she's got big and she's walking and talking. We celebrated her second birthday this year.

'We went around Dublin for the day, had a meal then we went to this big toy store in Tallaght called Smiths and I bought her an electric Barbie jeep. One of these power-driven ones. So I got her one of those. I also bought her a load of stuff over in England. She has more than any child I know and probably a little too much. It's because she's the only one, she's the only grandchild on both sides and everybody dotes over her and everybody buys her this that and the other. She'll end up getting too much and becoming spoilt and people won't want her so that's what we have to watch out for now. She's a great kid though, a great happy little child.'

Mikey isn't too keen on nappy-changing, though. 'It was a bit hard in the beginning as I don't have a very strong stomach for that kind of stuff,' he says. 'Sharon does most of it. If I have to do it I'll go in and do it, I won't refuse to do it. But if there's somebody else who offers to take on the task I'll let them go ahead.'

Mikey admits he sometimes finds it difficult to switch back from being a Boyzone star idolised by thousands of screaming girls at concerts around the world to normal family life.

'Yes it can be, because I find you are two different people,' he says. 'I've two separate lives and I play two separate roles, so obviously I look upon both of them differently. The pressure of changing from one to the other, chopping and changing can be a bit stressful, I suppose. For the last four years we've been away constantly, so I would have been more in the role of the pop star bit. But now I get home a lot more often because, as a result of the level of our success, we can choose to do quality rather than quantity of work. Do more high profile stuff rather than just doing everything for the sake of doing it. So due to that I get home a lot more often. I find it a lot easier to relax as a result.

'I experience more of the normal lifestyle now. I feel now I am back in the other seat, being in this life more. It's great because it ensures that my feet are firmer on the ground and I'm happy and relaxed in the knowledge that everything is OK at home.'

Although the house is set off by a large lawn, Mikey admits that he seldom turns his hand to gardening. 'No not at the moment, I have a gardener who looks after the garden for me,' he says. 'Basically it's a lawn and I have all these trees planted around the perimeter of my land. On a nice day I just like to potter around the place with me two German Pointer dogs and I'll do this, that and the other. Basically just relaxing and chilling out.'

As he drives around his neighbourhood in his sleek, black BMW, Mikey reflects on the dramatic change in his life and lifestyle during the last few years.

Stopping at the gates of St. David's secondary school on Dublin's Malahide Road, Mikey recalled how he dreamed of a life in the world of music when he was a student there. 'I was always into music and I knew that's what I would be doing at the end of the day,' he says.

"But I knew I had to try and make a living from something else first, until I became famous and successful. So I decided to become a mechanic. It was the only thing I was interested in...cars and that kind of stuff. I then served me time as a mechanic. That sounds like a prison sentence!'

Looking through the gates, Mikey suddenly realises just how far his career has taken him in a few short years, but his memories of school are mainly happy ones. He says: 'I was a decent pupil, but I wasn't an "A" sort. I was OK, but it's funny now to see a picture of myself on that school wall. It says something like, "Michael Graham, one of our past pupils, a Grade A student" and all that stuff. I helped them out a while ago. One of my old maths teachers came up to my house and he asked if I would help out with a school magazine they were doing. So I helped them out with that. It was for a brochure they were making to interest newcomers into the school.

'When I look at that school building I get shivers down my spine. They were all happy memories there. I get the shivers because of a reality, "God I used to go there." It was a whole different life to me at that time. And that's what it's like. It's like a very strong reminder of the past. Not that it's a bad past, but the realisation of the life I lived then and the life I live now. Somewhere down the line reality and fantasy cross-wired.'

Mikey grew up in the Dublin northside suburb of Coolock and as he returns he finds the place is changing. 'I have all good memories here as a child. But there was a playground across the road there from my mother's where I used to play all the time with all the other kids and now everything is gone out of the playground. All that's there now is an empty space with tar macadam and railings around it. So it's a bit sad really to see that happen to the area.'

Mikey has maintained strong links with his area by sponsoring a local soccer club and they now proudly wear his name on their jerseys. He says, 'The idea came about for that after Shane sponsored a soccer club in England...a kids team. There was a bit of a hullabaloo over here with people saying why couldn't he support an Irish team. I always had it in my head to do it and then one day I was down in the local pub and I got talking to the guy who is the manager of the local soccer team and I suggested sponsorship to him. He said that they needed it. It was just the right time because they were trying to buy new equipment. So I was happy to do it and they got a lot of publicity out of it and they were very happy. Since then they are at the top of the league and they reckon they're going to win the cup. It's great to be still involved in the community. It kind of helps from the aspect of people having respect for you in the area.'

A sports club not far from his family home in Coolock also stirs the memory bank as he recalls the days when he trained there as a kick-boxer. This year Mikey played a cameo role as a baddie in a martial arts movie. His character was a drug-dealing kidnapper

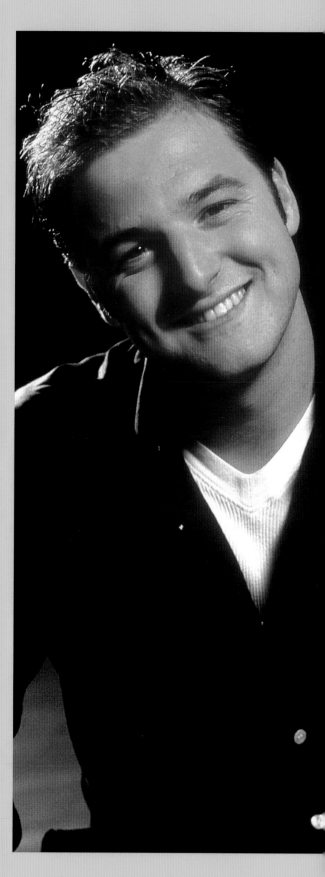

in the Bruce Lee-style flick *Fatal Deviation* and is the first martial arts film ever to be made in Ireland. Mikey acted in the movie completely free of charge because it's an amateur production that a friend of his, Peter Crinion, worked on. 'I always thought that one day I'd like to do a bit of acting and working on this film turned out to be a great experience,' he says.

'It's not a long movie, as far as I know it's only a half hour or forty minutes long. He plans to take it to Hong Kong and LA to have it screened over there. Maybe it could be made into a bigger-budget film.'

As he tours the streets of his own area, Mikey is instantly recognised. 'I am treated very good here,' he reveals as he acknowledges the people who wave to him. 'I am treated with a lot of respect. I am treated as a normal bloke by the people I know. The people who don't know me in the area are probably in shock when they bump into me, it's like "There he is, real flesh and blood." But I don't wander around here that much these days because I've moved out.'

While he plays a little golf for relaxation when he's off, Mikey's main pastime is cars. 'I like to tinker with cars. At the beginning of May I bought an old Ford Cortina for £150 so I'm that up as a project. You can't take the mechanic out of the man? I really enjoy that. I see it as a bit of a challenge, but an enjoyable one. I stick it in my own garage and work away on it. I still have all my tools and toolbox from the days when I was a mechanic. You never now, I might have to switch my hand back to it at some stage so I keep them handy. I don't mind getting grease under the fingernails. But if I ever have to go back to it, I'll be charging a high rate because I'm a good mechanic.'

Mikey's BMW is one of his prized possessions as well as a Harley Davidson motorbike and a KMX 125 scrambling bike. 'I love to do a bit of scrambling around the fields here at my home. I find it very relaxing,' he says.

The success of Boyzone has given Mikey a lifestyle that would otherwise have been just a dream. But he does find the lack of privacy that goes with stardom a little difficult to handle. 'It's the downside to success,' he says. 'The whole thing of walking down the street – though you may not be noticed or people may not come up to you – it's the feeling that all eyes are looking at you. I don't think I'll ever get used to being stared at.

'But generally I can move around freely in Dublin with Sharon and Hannah. If there's something that we want to do, like shopping, we don't go on a Saturday afternoon when the city is full of kids, we go on a Monday morning when there's nobody there. You just have to pick your times differently. We have to work around it in a different way. That's the price of being able to have a nice car, a nice house and live in the countryside. It's not a big price and as time goes on it will become easier.'

magic moments

i t was early evening in February and Boyzone's manager Louis Walsh was busy pouring through faxes, plotting the band's 1998 tour schedule and answering a never-ending stream of business calls at his Dublin headquarters.

The general requests and offers on the phones were the type to which the Boyzone guru has become accustomed. TV moguls were on the line trying to secure the Boyz for their shows. Magazine editors were seeking interviews for cover features.

Louis dealt with them all in his own inimitable style and with a degree of efficiency and professionalism that has helped the Boyz achieve their phenomenal success.

Amid the flurry of phone calls was one that took Louis completely by surprise. 'You want him to do what?' the Boyzone manager asked in disbelief. He listened wide-eyed as the local government chief relayed the details.

'Well, I'll have to ask him, but I'm sure he'll be very interested,' Louis replied.

I was in the office at the time, working on this new Boyzone book. Louis turned to me and said, 'They want Ronan to be the Grand Marshal for next month's St. Patrick's Day parade here in Dublin. Can you believe it?'

Ronan was beside himself with excitement when Louis phoned to pass on the news. Although he had received many amazing offers in his eventful career, this was something special.

To have the distinction of leading the historic St. Patrick's Day parade, which honours the country's patron saint every March 17, is the ultimate accolade for a native of Ireland.

The eyes of the world are on the country they call the Emerald Isle that day and everyone around the globe becomes an honorary Irish person for hours and hours of fun and frolics.

The parade also gave Ronan the ideal opportunity to unwrap his birthday present and take it out for a drive. The Boyzone star was in seventh heaven on March 17 as he sat behind the wheel of his convertible classic Ford Mustang car and headed up the Mardi Gras-style festival of colourful performers and marching bands through the streets of Dublin.

Half a million people turned out along the streets of the Irish capital to watch the spectacle of fun and fantasy in the two-mile parade and millions tuned in to it on TV around the world.

Ronan was accompanied in the car by Keith from Boyzone, his brother Gerard and his DJ pal Tony Fenton, of the Irish pop radio station 2FM.

Tony revealed, 'A few years ago the Irish soccer team were in the World Cup and while they didn't win, they gave a heroic performance that captured the imagination of the nation. As a result, Ireland gave them a heroes' welcome, with thousands lining the streets to welcome them home. The St. Patrick's Day parade was like that for Ronan and Keith. I was in the car with them and Ronan was saying, "This is what the Irish players must have felt like." It was absolutely mind-blowing.'

Ronan says; 'St Patrick's Day was something else. To be asked to do something like that in my home town was extra special. I'd done the MTV Awards and all that, but to be able to come home and be Grand Marshal of the St. Patrick's Day parade was an amazing feeling. It was a total honour and I thank the people of Ireland for accepting me in that way. People say we are ambassadors for our country, but that was the greatest honour for me to come home and do that. I would gladly be an ambassador for my country any day. I am honoured to be Irish and to be able to spread the word around.

'It was an amazing feeling that day that I could drive down the street and people weren't slagging me or calling me names. They were clapping their hands, saying "Go on, fair play to you". And Duster [Keith] came in the car with me. It was cool, we had such a laugh.

'Later I had the honour of singing for the Irish President Mary McAleese at Aras an Uachtaráin [the presidential residence] in Dublin's Phoenix Park. It's amazing to be seen in this light now because the band was slagged off when we started out, people gave us a hard time and now we're being respected finally. It's such a brilliant feeling. It's something we've worked hard for for years and we're finally getting that respect and it's wonderful. We thank the people for giving it to us.'

Keith says:, 'The St. Patrick's Day Parade was great fun. Initially we were kind of worried that we might get stones thrown at us because we were in a convertible car, but it was actually a fantastic feeling.'

Previously Ronan's biggest Irish honour was being voted Ireland's Entertainer Of The Year 1997 last Christmas by the public. 'That was so, so special to me,' he says. Ronan dedicated the award live on TV to his Mum, who was seriously ill at the time. His voice cracked as he spoke the words, 'This one is for you, Mam.'

Stephen realised two dreams last year by personally meeting his idol Michael Jackson in Dublin and singing on the

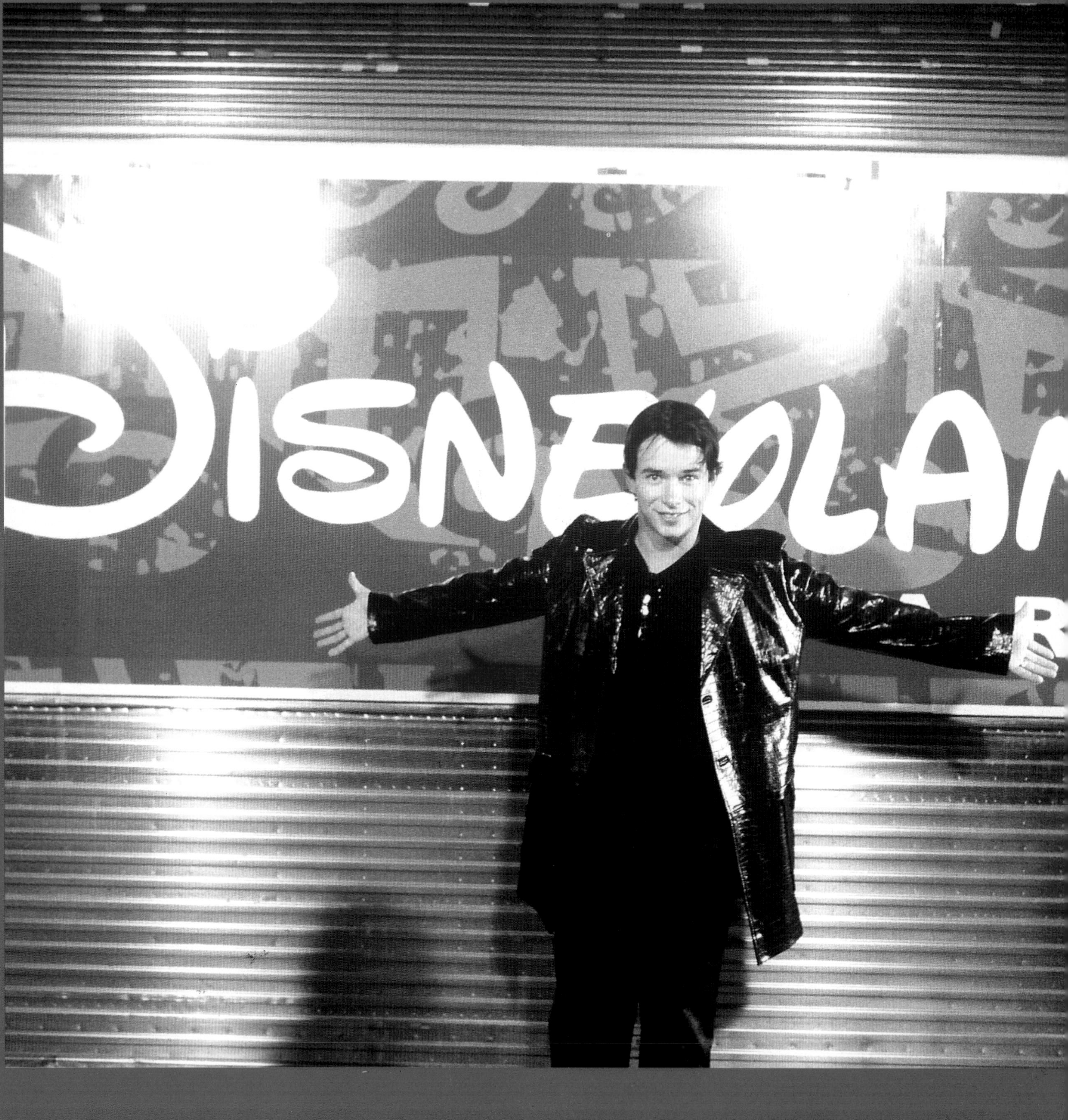

soundtrack of the Disney animated movie *Hercules*. He was the star guest at the UK charity première of *Hercules*, arriving outside the Odeon in London's Leicester Square aboard his own personal horse-drawn Roman chariot where he performed a live rendition of 'Shooting Star' to a screaming crowd of thousands. He attended several premières of the movie around Europe and also got the opportunity to sing 'Shooting Star' live on stage at Disneyland in Paris. But he was disappointed when it wasn't included on the soundtrack of the video, Disney used Michael Bolton's version instead. He says, 'I'm gutted over that because I thought I was going to have a personal Disney souvenir that would be with me for the rest of my life.'

After the Eurovision Song Contest, hosting the MTV Europe Music Awards in Rotterdam last November was another highlight of Ronan's career and he turned in a jaw-dropping performance in front of a TV audience of one billion people. And he did it in the middle of Boyzone's Something Else UK tour, flying back and forth from Britain to Rotterdam every night to rehearse.

Ronan says, 'It was worth it. Opening the show was a rush. It was mind-blowing walking out on stage with the crowd going mental, that was fantastic. I enjoyed the whole thing and afterwards I partied until daylight. Then I was back in Cardiff doing the Boyzone show the next night. It was a mad, mad time.'

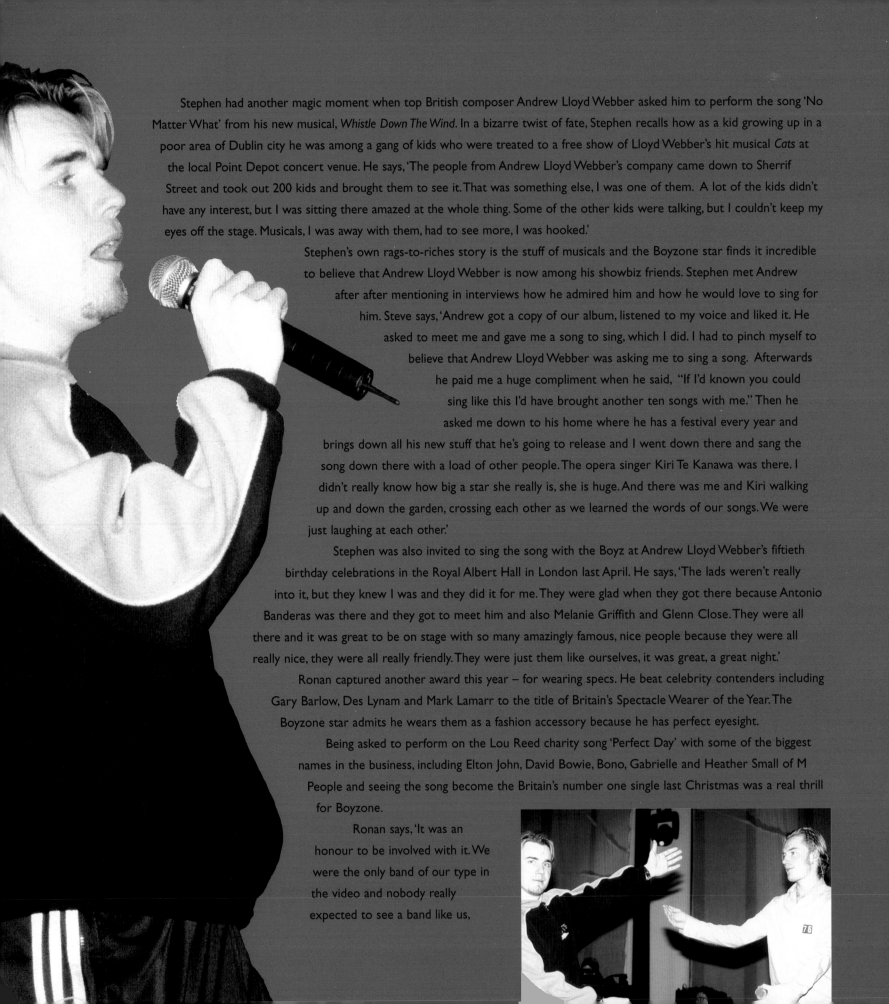

Stephen had another magic moment when top British composer Andrew Lloyd Webber asked him to perform the song 'No Matter What' from his new musical, *Whistle Down The Wind*. In a bizarre twist of fate, Stephen recalls how as a kid growing up in a poor area of Dublin city he was among a gang of kids who were treated to a free show of Lloyd Webber's hit musical *Cats* at the local Point Depot concert venue. He says, 'The people from Andrew Lloyd Webber's company came down to Sherrif Street and took out 200 kids and brought them to see it. That was something else, I was one of them. A lot of the kids didn't have any interest, but I was sitting there amazed at the whole thing. Some of the other kids were talking, but I couldn't keep my eyes off the stage. Musicals, I was away with them, had to see more, I was hooked.'

Stephen's own rags-to-riches story is the stuff of musicals and the Boyzone star finds it incredible to believe that Andrew Lloyd Webber is now among his showbiz friends. Stephen met Andrew after after mentioning in interviews how he admired him and how he would love to sing for him. Steve says, 'Andrew got a copy of our album, listened to my voice and liked it. He asked to meet me and gave me a song to sing, which I did. I had to pinch myself to believe that Andrew Lloyd Webber was asking me to sing a song. Afterwards he paid me a huge compliment when he said, "If I'd known you could sing like this I'd have brought another ten songs with me." Then he asked me down to his home where he has a festival every year and brings down all his new stuff that he's going to release and I went down there and sang the song down there with a load of other people. The opera singer Kiri Te Kanawa was there. I didn't really know how big a star she really is, she is huge. And there was me and Kiri walking up and down the garden, crossing each other as we learned the words of our songs. We were just laughing at each other.'

Stephen was also invited to sing the song with the Boyz at Andrew Lloyd Webber's fiftieth birthday celebrations in the Royal Albert Hall in London last April. He says, 'The lads weren't really into it, but they knew I was and they did it for me. They were glad when they got there because Antonio Banderas was there and they got to meet him and also Melanie Griffith and Glenn Close. They were all there and it was great to be on stage with so many amazingly famous, nice people because they were all really nice, they were all really friendly. They were just them like ourselves, it was great, a great night.'

Ronan captured another award this year – for wearing specs. He beat celebrity contenders including Gary Barlow, Des Lynam and Mark Lamarr to the title of Britain's Spectacle Wearer of the Year. The Boyzone star admits he wears them as a fashion accessory because he has perfect eyesight.

Being asked to perform on the Lou Reed charity song 'Perfect Day' with some of the biggest names in the business, including Elton John, David Bowie, Bono, Gabrielle and Heather Small of M People and seeing the song become the Britain's number one single last Christmas was a real thrill for Boyzone.

Ronan says, 'It was an honour to be involved with it. We were the only band of our type in the video and nobody really expected to see a band like us,

Boyzone, in a video of that calibre. But for us it was credible to be in it and the people that were on it like, David Bowie, Bono, Elton John, everybody that's anybody in the music industry, we were so very proud to be in among them. We're proud that people would give us the opportunity to do it. It's obvious that people look at us in a different light to the rest of the bands that are around in our category. And being number one on Christmas Day, it was unbelievable, absolutely brilliant, an amazing feeling.'

Boyzone recorded their segment of the 'Perfect Day' video on the last day of their UK tour in a studio next door to Wembley. Ronan says, 'We put down the vocal in the studio and they recorded the video bit in the same studio. It took two hours. We were wrapped in material like tin foil – black, hard tin foil. We were laughing, breaking our hearts laughing and we had to do it a few times and were sweating with all the lights and the metal. It was a good laugh.'

Ronan has enjoyed a couple of special moments performing on stage with Gary Barlow, the former Take That idol who has now become a close mate of the Boyzone star. They did a duet singing 'Harvest For The World' at the Concert of Hope down at Battersea Power Station last December. Then they teamed up again in Dublin last March. Ronan says, 'We arranged my guest spot with Gary when we met up at his Albert Hall show in London during March. Gary has been one of my idols from Take That days. He was a singer and songwriter I looked up to and still do. Joining Gary on stage in my own home town was really something special. We've become great pals in recent years and we have a lot in common at this stage of Boyzone's career. I can sit down with him now and discuss life in the hectic world of pop. We share experiences and learn from each other. On the day he performed in Dublin I joined him backstage during rehearsals for Sunday lunch. It was a bit of a reunion because Gary's bass player Paul also plays bass guitar on Boyzone's live shows. We both got a great buzz from the duet. I sat on the piano as Gary tinkled the ivories while we sang Elton John's 'Your Song' and we also performed 'Harvest For The World' and the home crowd was brilliant, the fans gave us a fantastic reception. Two of the boxes in the theatre were full with my family and friends so that was a bit special as well. Afterwards, Gary and I hit the town and really let our hair down. It was a great night out. He loves coming to Dublin.'

Stephen got a big surprise in April of this year when Geri Halliwell of the Spice Girls phoned him live on the BBC Radio 1 *Breakfast Show* to personally thank him for his advice on how to improve the SpiceWorld live show. He says, 'Ronan and I were on the breakfast show with Zoë Ball and we were both surprised when Geri phoned in to invite us to the Girls' party at Wembley. But I was really thrilled when she thanked me over the airwaves for all the tips I gave the girls after the opening of their world tour in The Point back home in Dublin. I went to The Point to review the Spice Girls show for GMTV when it was launched in February. The girls came up to me after the concert and they were asking, "What's the story? What did you think of the show? What did you like and what didn't you like?" I told them honestly what I thought of the production and the

performance and I gave my views on where they could make little changes and so on, but I never really thought that they paid any heed to it. Imagine my surprise then when Geri actually went on air and said, "Thanks very much for the tips." Wow! Fair play to them, they've done incredibly well and all the Boyz have become great mates with them.

One of the biggest surprises of 1998 for Ronan was winning an Ivor Novello Award, which is the Oscar of the music business. 'I only saw George Michael and Elton John and people like that getting this award,' he says. 'For Ronan Keating from the Northside of Dublin to be put up for this amazing writing award is just beyond anything I ever imagined. It's the greatest honour any writer can get in the world, so I was over the moon with joy.'

Performing at Wembley Arena in London is always a special time for Boyzone. It's not the biggest venue on their tour, but it's the one every group wants to play. It was there that their Irish radio DJ pal Tony Fenton got the opportunity to experience life in the hottest pop band on the planet.

He reveals, 'I was with them for two Wembley shows and I travelled to the venue in their blacked out van. As we got closer to the stadium the sound of fans screaming was unreal. When the van turned the top of the road into view of the screaming fans the noise was deafening. Getting out of the van with the guys was amazing and security whisked us into venue amid a euphoric atmosphere.

'I was surprised by how much goes into each show. You would think that the boys come in, do their gig and go away. But there's a lot of work behind the scenes and a lot of people involved. There's a guy assigned to look after the microphones, a guy looking after drum sound...there are about forty people backstage running around.

'I also realised that there's an incredible amount of work involved in being a pop star. I flew over with Ronan and we were both hungover because we'd been out on the town in Dublin the night before. We were picked up at Heathrow Airport and got to our hotel about 1pm. He said, "I'll see you in reception about 4.30pm." He went upstairs and had a quick shower, then he had an interview with MTV...RTE TV from Ireland were over and he had to do an interview with them...there were three radio stations to do interviews with...there was a photo session with a magazine...another photo session for their own *Boyzone* magazine. I was relaxing in my room, but Ronan had all those things to get done before the show that night.

'I went down to look at a couple of photo sessions and Ronan and the Boyz were still there...Ro was still smiling, still maintaining his level of enthusiasm and I thought that was unbelievable. And all that was before the show later that evening. No one really knows the amount of commitments they have. There are radio interviews, TV interviews and photo sessions, one after another every day. That day wasn't too bad because they were all in the same building. The next day we went off in the van to another photo shoot, left there and drove a mile or two down the road to do another shoot in another studio and it was constantly changing clothes and not eating the right food and all of that. It's tough. It might look glamorous when they are on the covers of all the glossy magazines, but it's a tough gig. But they wouldn't change it. They love what they do, you'd have to to keep up that pace.'

a charity fashion show in Dublin three years ago sparked off one of pop's hottest romances that this year led to Boyzone heart-throb Shane Lynch marrying stunning Eternal singer Easther Bennett.

Eternal were among the guests at the star-studded event that included Supermodels like Naomi Campbell and Eva Hertzigova. Boyzone were also on the catwalk that night and Shane realised that he was deeply attracted to Easther. Their eyes met and there was an instant spark.

Shane says, 'I think that's the first time we kind of clicked. I had met Esther a few times before that, but we only said hellos and goodbyes.'

Their romance, however, got off to a shaky start when Shane decided to ask Easther for a date...and she refused! 'That day I actually asked her out to dinner and she said "No" – she turned me down simply because she thought I was joking. I learned this later when we finally got together and you tell each other how you felt. Easther said that from the very start she was absolutely crazy about me, but she said "No" because she thought I was winding her up and that I wasn't serious.

'But after that we exchanged numbers and she was on tour in the UK and I happened to be around at the time in Birmingham, and they were performing in Birmingham and they came down to the hotel

ane

and we played cards and became really good friends. Then one day when I was on tour with Boyzone I asked her out, I asked her to date me as they say, and she had no objections whatsoever and it went from there. I knew she was the one for me and vice versa and I asked her to marry me. I got down on one knee and I asked her to be me wife.'

The stunning couple's fairytale wedding on Sunday, March 8, was held in the magnificent 500-year-old Leez Priory and was strictly controlled to ensure that it was a private affair. Journalists and photographer were kept at bay by a top-notch security team led by Boyzone's chief of security Barrie Knight, and guests were asked not to bring cameras or video recorders.

Shane revealed, 'It was our wedding and our day and we wanted to keep it as private as possible. I didn't even admit I was dating Easther until I actually got married. To be honest, I feel it's nobody's business but ours. I'm happy to say the wedding was everything I could have hoped for, it was really special. We did the whole thing according to the rules, traditionally as they say, where you get engaged and then the next year you get married and that's the way we planned things and that's exactly how it went.

'The wedding ceremony was absolutely beautiful. I can't speak for anybody else where marriage is concerned, but it's something I could never ever explain to anyone. It's such a special day and if you want to feel that, you have to get married yourself. When two people are completely in love and you go through that motion where you can't get any closer other than being married, well that's the most amazing experience you will ever have.

'I was surrounded by a lot of people, a lot of friends and family, but you're on such a high you don't notice all the people around you. Everyone could have been there, but they may as well not have been there. It's you and your wife's day and you don't bother about anybody else.

'The wedding ceremony itself was far from ordinary and traditional. I was dressed in red, a long red jacket and Easther's style was Indian, she had all the gold, like the rings, chains and bracelets, a nose-chain to her ear, all very Indian, and she was also in red. She was the most beautiful woman I ever saw in my life on that day, absolutely amazing.'

After taking their official vows before a registrar, Shane and Easther's marriage was then blessed by her mother, who is a pastor. The couple spent a week-long honeymoon in South Africa.

The happy couple now live in a five-bedroomed English mansion set in twenty acres of land. Shane admits that he's a house proud hubby who loves gardening and tending to his fishponds. 'I'm into my ponds,' he reveals. 'I have lots of water works around me. I'm big into my fish at the moment...fish and gardening and all of that, it's now a bigger passion than bikes. I need something to relax with and I think fish are the most amazing thing ever. I have a fifteen-foot aquarium in my house.'

One of the features of Shane's new home is a recording studio, but that's exclusively for the benefit of Easther because the Boyzone star has no ambitions to pursue music after the supergroup. 'I'm not into doing my own recording or music,' he says. 'That is there for my wife, that's her deal, it's nothing to do with me.'

Shane's favourite 'room' in the house is the garage. 'I have all my cars, tools and bikes in it. There's a Porsche, a BMW, five Toyotas, two of which are trucks, two Corolla rally cars and a front-wheel-drive Corolla, which is a runaround. I have a four-wheel- drive track around my land. And then there's my motorbikes and I have a motorcross track on my land as well.'

It's a lifestyle that Shane <u>knew</u> as a teenager he would one day enjoy. As he takes a trip in his Porsche around the area where he grew up, Shane stops outside Grange Community College and recalls his dreams and ambitions when he was a student there. 'To be honest. I didn't have any dreams about becoming a singer in a pop group,' he says. 'I always said that before I was twenty years old I would have a Porsche, that's one thing I said to all my mates in school and I fulfilled that dream when I was nineteen. And I said before I was twenty-two I would be married and I did that when I was twenty-one. I didn't know how I was going to get the Porsche or didn't know who I was going to marry, but I always said that's what I would do.

'Standing outside that College looking in today, I can honestly say that my days there were happy. It was an absolutely brilliant time, simply to do with the few people from my class that I happened to hang around with way back then. I always got on well with the teachers, no problems, they always let me do my own thing. I never got into any grief or hassle until I got to third year and the main man, the Principal as they say, just asked me

not to come back after the summer holidays because he felt I was wasting my time there and that's why I actually left school.'

A cruise to the local Father Collins' Park reveals how the young Shane Lynch used to hang out there while skipping off school. 'We used to go down there on our motorbikes,' he says. 'We wouldn't bother going to school, we'd just get the motorbike out of the garage and push it down there and spend all day in the park mitching. If my father knew what I got up to at the time I'd be crucified. It was my own motorbike which I had from the time I was fourteen years old. It had been my Da's from years and years ago, an old scrambler, he never did anything with them so myself and the boys did it up and started riding it. We all had our bikes at the time.'

Shane zips around to McDonald's in Donaghmede where he used to hang out in his later teens. 'It was when we first got our cars and it was a bit of a hang out area...everyone met in McDonald's.'

But the main landmark in Shane's life at that stage was St. Anne's Park in Raheny. 'We had a place called Chucky's and that's something we built with our bare hands in the park to mess around with our bikes and there it still stands to this day. Chucky's is a little place, on a corner of the park, it's the corner where the road goes out to Dollymount and we built ramps there and all kind of things for our bikes. It was our territory.'

As a teenager, Shane went to work in his Dad's garage, just like his sister Keavy from B*witched and some of his best memories are from that period. 'I worked there for two years before I left school. I was a petrol pump attendant,' he says. 'As a kid, I used to finish school at ten past four, run home, get changed and had to be in work for 5.30pm and I worked from 5.30pm to 11 o'clock at night and it was hard work to be honest, but I was a kid and earned a few pounds at the end of the week and it was absolutely brilliant. Then when I left school, or was asked to leave school, I went to work there before I joined Boyzone.'

Looking back, it seems like a million years ago, but Shane admits he would have no problem taking up where he left off at his Dad's garage. Working as a mechanic still gives him a major thrill. 'To be honest, I think I could adapt back to those surroundings very, very easily because having to deal with cars is something I really love doing and to adapt back to it would not be any problem whatsoever. Maybe the money and the wages might have a bit of a bearing on the matter, but I could definitely go back to the lifestyle.'

The Ormond Centre in Dublin is where Boyzone was born. It was the venue where the auditions for the supergroup were held. All the aspiring young Irish pop stars queued up to join the band that was set to conquer the world. It was an exciting period with the media focusing in on the search for Ireland's answer to Take That. Shane Lynch was among the Boyzone line up from its inception because, he says, the band was his idea to begin with and it was he who approached their manager Louis Walsh. 'I was the one who said, "Let's get this together." At the end of the day, the Ormond was something I went to, to watch people audition.'

Boyzone's success takes the group all over the world and has introduced the individual members to countries that they had previously associated with their geography class at school. In Shane's case, Portugal had been part of his childhood years long before Boyzone became a household name. He says, 'Every summer our family used to go there for two months. I made friends there throughout that time, but in two months you don't get too close to people. At the end of the day, I always looked forward to coming home to my real mates. Although it was an amazing experience to go to Portugal for two months.'

On tour with Boyzone, Shane is usually the one member who retires early to his hotel room. You will rarely find him in the bar and that may be the effect of a distasteful experience he had when he was a teenager on holiday in Portugal. 'I got really drunk on holiday in Portugal when I was about fourteen years old and I've never forgotten the experience,' he says. 'I was with my cousin and one of my other mates and we were all in Portugal on holiday with my parents. At the age of fourteen you're not allowed to drink so we, being the lads that we thought we were, were in a pub having a laugh. We were racing beer to see who could drink them the fastest. I suppose we had three or four pints in the space of twenty minutes. My sister also had a bottle of Malibu stashed outside the pub for a beach party that had been planned. She asked me to bring it to her, but we drank that as well and then we went to meet her and told her that the bottle had been stolen. As soon as I sat down next to her — it was like a switch — it all came over me at the same time. I got up from the chair and staggered to the back of a beach hut and sat against a boat before lying on the sand. I was in a terrible state. I couldn't move. I had to be dragged home — it was disgusting. I haven't been drunk since.'

This year Shane's life has changed dramatically as he finds himself juggling life as a young married man with that of a busy pop star. But, in keeping with the laid-back nature of the guy, he's taking it all in his stride. 'I know Easther is always there for me and she's always in my heart and in my mind. Of course, I would like her there in body too, but love goes beyond all of that and you can get over that once you know the situation in your relationship and I know I am completely secure in that. There are no problems. I am completely proud of Easther and I just love her to bits. She's not my girlfriend anymore, she's my wife, that's something I am very proud of.'

top of the pops

i t was just a few days before the official start of summer 1998 and Boyzone were gearing up for a chart attack.

With a new album waiting in the wings, the Boyz had released 'All That I Need' as a taster for their album. The performance of their first 1998 release and the reaction from fans would indicate their popularity on the music scene as they cranked up their hit machine for the fifth year of their roller-coaster ride through the wacky showbiz scene.

In the fickle world of pop, no band ever takes their success for granted. Stardom is not an everlasting gift and going into a new year with a new single and album, Boyzone were on tenterhooks.

Prior to the launch of their first single of the year, the lads had an early morning start one day and spent several hours on the rooftop of a very high London building in wet and windy conditions during a two-day shoot for the video of 'All That I Need'.

Boyzone magazine editor Allison Maund reveals, 'The Boyz looked gorgeous in their brand-new, hand made, real leather red suits on the set of "All That I Need". There was loads of waiting around for shooting to start, but Ro and Steve relieved the boredom by playing on the studio computer game.

'Stephen was miffed because he had to arrive at the studio so early in the morning. Ro was complaining about the cold and the rain outside, then disappeared back inside like a big girl.

'Steve broke the director's chair accidentally, but Shane fixed it in a very professional fashion. Ronan took a special liking to the video set's showbiz table and wanted to steal it for his new house.

'Mikey and Stephen's feet were hurting because of their brand new shoes, so they were eventually allowed to wear much more comfy sandals instead because nobody can see their feet in the closing scenes.

'Ro's turn-ups on his trousers kept falling down and had to be re-stuck with Copydex, while Stephen used the glue to try to stick Alex the stylist's bottles to a table.

'At the end of day one, poor old Ro waited around for ages not realising that his shots had actually already finished for the day half an hour before.

'The filming on the second day was inside the building where All Saints shot their "I Know Where It's At" video.'

It was Sunday evening on April 26, 1998, and Stephen was lined up for an interview with British DJ Dr Fox of Capital Radio, who was counting down the official charts.

The mid-week sales had been promising, placing Boyzone at number one ahead of the Run DMC vs Jason Nevins hit, 'It's Like That', which had dominated the top position for weeks.

Stephen was anxiously tapping his feet and fiddling with the buttons on his shirt as the show entered the top five. He was too terrified to tempt fate by daring to believe that Boyzone had toppled 'It's Like That'.

The whoops of joy from Stephen that greeted listeners to the show when Dr Fox announced that Boyzone had scored their first number one hit of 1998 with 'All That I Need' was a totally genuine reaction.

It was a huge sense of relief for all the Boyz. Getting to number one position in the charts is still a major buzz for Ronan, Stephen, Shane, Mikey and Keith.

Hitting the top spot is a reflection of the group's popularity and a tremendous boost of confidence for the Boyz themselves. The previous day, Larry Gogan, the doyen of Irish DJs, also had the Boyz tuned in to his chart show on 2FM Radio as they waited for the announcement of Ireland's top-selling single of the week. Once again, they had reasons to celebrate as 'All That I Need' came in at the pole position.

Success in their own country was even sweeter for the Boyz. Ireland may not be the biggest market in the world, but it's where they come from and they crave respect from their own people. Ronan has openly admitted that he's been deeply hurt and offended by the negative attitudes Boyzone have

'Our singles didn't go in at number one in the early days, we climbed the charts the whole way up.'

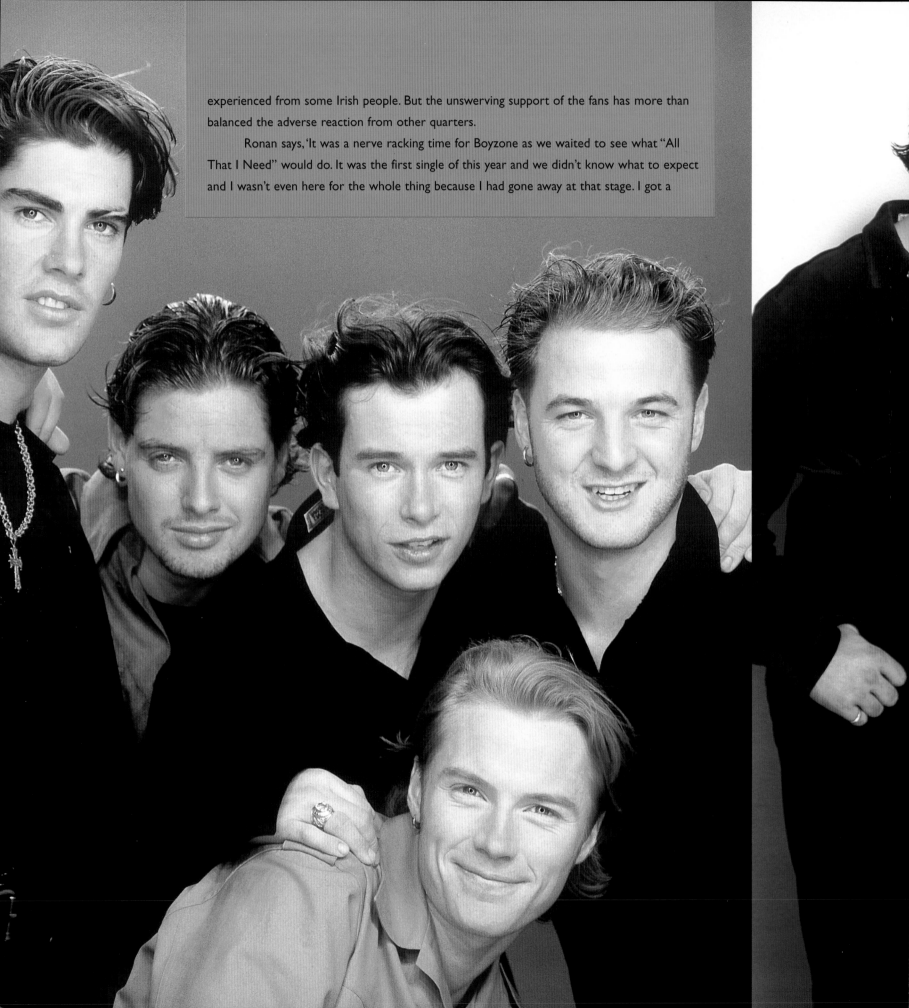

experienced from some Irish people. But the unswerving support of the fans has more than balanced the adverse reaction from other quarters.

Ronan says, 'It was a nerve racking time for Boyzone as we waited to see what "All That I Need" would do. It was the first single of this year and we didn't know what to expect and I wasn't even here for the whole thing because I had gone away at that stage. I got a

phone call to say we were number one and what a brilliant feeling it was to be back up there and still be wanted by our fans. It was a great start for the album as well.

'Our singles didn't go in at number one in the early days, we climbed the charts the whole way up. All the other bands, without mentioning names, who came in at number one, have to live up to that all the time. But for a band like us, we went straight in at number ten, then to two, and all the time we were two, threes and fours and then finally we got our first number one with 'Words' and then we got our second with 'A Different Beat' and then we went back down to twos and threes and then back in again at number one. I think it has been very consistent and for us that's an amazing thing, that's not a usual pop phenomenon...we've stood the test of time.'

Keith says, 'Getting to number one with 'All That I Need' at the start of the year was a fantastic feeling, more than anyone realises...for the simple reason that we're a pop group and people put a time limit on pop groups and it's like you feel you have to justify yourself to please everybody and to get another number one five years on. It's great that we're still pulling them out of the bag and we have enjoyed our biggest year yet. It was also the first number one we had in Ireland in a while, so it was a new lease of life and, hopefully, it sets us up for another few years.'

Steve says, 'Getting to number one is always exciting for us. I don't believe for a minute that it's any different for other bands. On the day of the charts you're saying, "I hope it's number one". All that week I was saying, "I hope it's number one", to Shane and the rest of the lads...and then you hit the jackpot. It gets to number one and it gives everyone a boost. Everyone in the band got a lift, you get a lift because you know then your hard work is paying off and that what you're doing is good and people are enjoying it. That just helps you a lot, it really does.'

Stephen was also thrilled to discover that Boyzone had broken Kylie Minogue's record for scoring the biggest number of continuous top five hits in the UK with their eleven top-five singles. They've scored even more success in their native Ireland where they also had a top five hit with their debut single, 'Working My Way Back To You'. Steve says, 'We have a record now, we have the same record as Kylie Minogue and that's an achievement when you consider how big and how famous she was in her heyday.'

Shane says, 'Getting to number one with 'All That I Need' was one that meant most to me because our first number one was kind of expected nearly and then our second one kind of went with the flow, but then we missed two in between that, so the third one was very very special to me. I feel very proud of having that number one. I really realised what we had because we missed the other two, so it was actually brilliant.'

Reflecting on their success, Mikey recalled their struggle to make an impact at home in the lead with their first single, 'Working My Way Back To You', which was released in Ireland back in May 1994, and entered the chart at number two. He says, 'We did go through hell to get here. If anyone thinks Boyzone started off with a bang, became huge and millionaires overnight, they're greatly mistaken. We went through a year and a half of hard graft around Ireland before we went to England. The reception we got was often very demoralising. It was degrading going into clubs around our own country, doing our little bit and having people throwing ice, glasses, cigarettes and spitting and hurling abuse. We went through all that, but we kept together and we made it and turned out to be happy men with a few bob in our pockets.'

Their breakthrough song in Britain was 'Love Me For A Reason', which went to number one in Ireland and entered the UK chart at number ten, finishing up at number two behind East 17's 'Stay Another Day' at Christmas 1994.

Since then their hit machine has churned out top-selling singles 'Key To My Life', 'So Good', 'Father and Son', 'Coming Home', 'Words', 'A Different Beat', 'Isn't It A Wonder', 'Picture of You', 'Baby Can I Hold You', 'All That I Need'.

Monday, May 20, 1998, was another landmark in the career of Boyzone...it heralded the birth of their new 'baby' called *Where We Belong*, the follow up to their 2.2 million-selling album, *A Different Beat*.

Months of work behind the scenes had gone in to the package of fifteen songs that the Boyz finally unveiled on *Where We Belong*.

Stephen says, 'I love my two songs, "You Flew Away" and "Where Did You Go?", on this album. I wrote them for everybody else, not for me. I wrote them for people who suffer the loss of somebody close to them, whether it's someone passing away or somebody in a

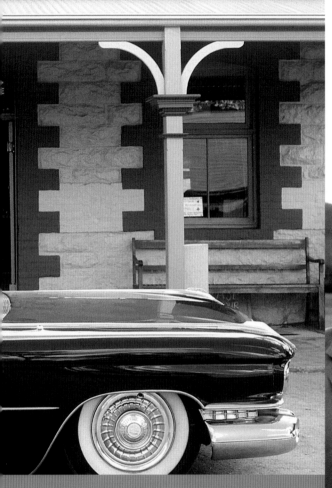

relationship walking out. I wanted the lyrics to be subtle so that they're not negative, but have a positive vibe and offer hope. The melodies are all very uplifting and at the end of "You Flew Away" I brought in a really strong Gospel choir. It's a song that starts off quite slow, quite relaxed and it builds and builds. I got a guy called Johnny Douglas to produce that and he produced "Fast Love" for George Michael. He did an incredible job.

'Then I wrote "Where Did You Go?" and it's pretty much something similar, it's very uplifting, very catchy. It's Shane's favourite song of the album, he likes it best. Everyone else seemed to like it as well. Ronan's stuff is just incredible, the stuff that he has written. You can

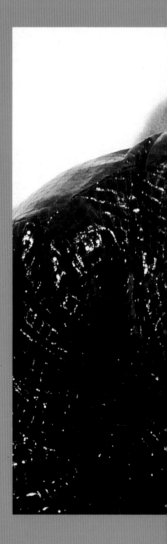

see that he is just getting better and better at writing, we all are. Myself and Ro do a lot of writing, we love being in the studio. He wrote "I Must Have Been High". It's a great song, it's a dancey song, a really, really killer song and I love it. I did a huge amount of backing vocals on this album and I'm delighted with that. People, when they hear the album, they say "There's Stephen, there's Stephen" in the songs.

'When I'm working on songs I don't write in the studio, mostly when I'm in there I'm singing. On "You Flew Away" I did every BV [backing vocal] on it, except for the gospel choir, and on "Where Did you Go?" I did the lead vocals and then I brought the rest of the lads in to do the backing vocals. I worked with the producers and they would say "What about this way?" and I'd say, "No, what about this way?" I know what I want when I am in the studio and I know what I want to hear. You've got to be in a creative mood and you've got to sit down and say, "Let's do this, let's try this, and that." You've got to have confidence and go for it, guide it and let the song make itself.'

The inspiration for songs come in many different ways and the tracks were written in various situations. Mikey tells how he wrote his song, "Good Conversation", which is track number thirteen on *Where We Belong*. He says, 'I didn't have to do too much thinking for that

one. It came to me one night lying in bed in my hotel room. I wrote the full song in about fifteen minutes or so. It's written from several angles. It's about love and how confusing it can be and how everybody is mixed up about love these days and the problems it causes. It's also about old friends treating you like you're new sometimes. They don't know how to handle your fame and really you're the same friend you've always been. It also refers to the record company and how fickle the whole pop industry is sometimes...it's good, but it's fake...it's a

good laugh, but you can't take it for real. If you do
that you're lost, you've got to keep your feet firmly
on the ground. Going in to the studio to record this
song was a really good time for me because I love
working in the studio and I wish I had more
opportunity to do it.'

As he relaxes and listens to the tracks on
Where We Belong, Ronan allows himself a satisfied
smile. 'It's a step ahead of the other two albums,' he
says. 'You need to progress with every album and
move on and that's what we've done with this album.
We've taken a step on, we co-produced and wrote
most of the album. It's an album about relationships
and feelings we've had since we were kids, our lives
and what we've gone through and our families and
friends.'

To celebrate the launch of their third album,
Boyzone threw a big showbiz bash in London's
Gatliff Road Depot, where a special fun fair, featuring
attractions like bumper cars and rifle ranges, created
a carnival atmosphere, in keeping with the Boyz' fun-
loving image.

The 500 guests entering the large warehouse
style venue were greeted by stilt-walking demons
breathing hell's fire and everyone tucked into good
old fashioned burgers, hot dogs and chips as they
waited for the Famous Five to make their entrance.
Candy floss was all part of the celebrations as well,
and all present were delighted when the Boyz
emerged from the VIP area, after their round of
photographs and interviews with the media from all
over Europe, to join in the spirit of the occasion by
going into battle in the bumper cars. Ronan and his
bride Yvonne were the centre of attention as they
shared a car among the mayhem in the ring. Mikey
later complained how his knees were aching after
taking a battering in his bumper from some lucky
young girl fans who'd managed to get their hands on
invitations to the special event.

The colourful crowd included several family members of Boyzone, including Keith's mum and dad, Sean and Pat, and his wife Lisa. Stephen's brother and sister, Tony and Michelle, also flew over from Dublin for the glittering event. Mikey was joined by his girlfriend Sharon and the happy couple announced their engagement on the night. Shane's sisters, Edele and Keavy from pop group B*Witched and Tara from Fab!, also turned up to support their famous brother.

There were a number of other well-known faces among the glitterati, including former models Sam Fox and Mandy Smith and the stars of bands like the Divine Comedy, UB40 and The Corrs. Guitarist Brian May of former supergroup Queen also turned up with his little daughter Emily, aged eleven, who introduced him to the music of Boyzone. Brian said, 'I hope to work with Boyzone. I love the band and Ronan is a star in any generation.'

Stephen is proud of the fact that Boyzone has now expanded its fan base with the album, *Where We Belong*, and he feels 'All That I Need' is a ballad that touched a chord with an older and new audience. He says, 'There seems to be a lot of other people buying our records now and they don't see us being this teen band, people who liked "All That I Need" like what we do now. I think that's been great for us and that helped us get number one and, hopefully, that will secure our future.'